THE
BLUE
RIBBON

Dear Blue Ribbon Member,

It is my pleasure to provide you a copy of "THE BLUE RIBBON: Amazing Women, Powerful Giving" in commemoration of The Blue Ribbon's 45th Anniversary.

This book is the work of co-chairs Donna Wolff and Betty Leonard, who took the idea of a short book in honor of Blue Ribbon's anniversary to a place beyond my wildest dreams. They found the book's author Betty Goodwin, hired publisher Angel City Press, and worked tirelessly for the last year to make this project an exceptional look at the past, present and future of The Blue Ribbon.

I also extend my deepest thanks to treasured longtime member, Dona Kendall, who generously gave the lead gift and helped make this book possible.

Finally, I thank you, Blue Ribbon's members. Your generous hearts, loving participation, and passionate support of the performing arts allow Blue Ribbon to continue to make a difference.

With gratitude,

Carla Sands
President, The Blue Ribbon

BLUE RIBBON

Amazing Women
Powerful Giving

BLUE RIBBON

Amazing Women
Powerful Giving

Betty Goodwin

Contents

INTRODUCTION

Like Mrs. Chandler,
**our members are on a course
to change lives and institutions**
and greatly enrich the culture of Los Angeles.

I n 1968, an amazing group of women came together to support the Music Center; and, indeed, those women were *truly* amazing.

Born in an era when women were not expected to lead, the women of the Blue Ribbon did exactly that. Inspired by the determination of Dorothy Buffum Chandler, the visionary who worked relentlessly to raise the necessary funds to construct the first three buildings that comprise the now-renowned Los Angeles performing arts center, these women of the Blue Ribbon found creative ways to help sustain the resident companies that are at the heart of this city, the true culture that emanates from the structures that embody the Music Center.

Five decades later, the Blue Ribbon continues, and the esteemed Dorothy Buffum Chandler remains as our inspiration. In these pages, you will learn how, for the first time in the history of Los Angeles, she brought together "old" society and "new" society, Eastside and Westside, unifying people of different social groups, businesses, religions, and political beliefs in a groundbreaking effort to support—and yes, to *impact*—the culture of our city; and how her vision and determination not only brought together Los Angeles to build the Music Center, but she encouraged women to find ways to expand upon her ideas and express themselves. As you turn the pages, you will witness the difference Blue Ribbon women have made throughout these many years.

The history of the Blue Ribbon reflects the changing role of women in our society. From its inception, Blue Ribbon members have been well-educated and well-intentioned. Today, in contrast to the original members of the group, almost all new members have worked in professions outside the home, and many are actively pursuing careers *and* devoting time to philanthropy. Blue Ribbon has adapted and will always adapt as our lives change with the times: women from dual-career households, working mothers, women living single lives, women keeping up with the speed of communication and technology. Blue Ribbon women are twenty-first-century women, meeting every new challenge, and yet sticking to the goals of supporting the culture and cultural heritage of Los Angeles.

Our mutual love of the arts brings us together to build lifelong connections and friendships, enriching and strengthening our own lives, as well as the lives of the citizens of Los Angeles and their children. Our annual Children's Festival instills the love of music, dance, and theater in new generations. As you will read, the Festival's history is fascinating. We welcome thousands of children to the Music Center annually, and each year I think of how much we learn from and about these young people. What a joy to be with them and to share our city's very best arts with all of them and their teachers.

The Festival also provides an opportunity to work together with our members. How wonderful for us to work side-by-side with many of this city's most influential women in philanthropy. Beyond the Music Center, our members have made important gifts to area hospitals, museums, universities, and children's causes and many other leading organizations and causes throughout the country and the world.

Our mandate as members is to continue the group's legacy as established by Mrs. Chandler and to expand our organization. We must work to increase our financial support of the resident companies and the performing arts at the Music Center, and encourage the women of Los Angeles to support each other and our evolving culture. It's my hope that with this historic book we look back and learn, and determine what we will take from the past, and imagine what we will create for the future. It also allows us to celebrate our accomplishments and informs our goals as we look ahead.

The Blue Ribbon membership has followed the extraordinary model set in place by Dorothy Buffum Chandler, welcoming outstanding women from all areas of greater Los Angeles and from a myriad of backgrounds—women who all want to make a difference. Like Mrs. Chandler, our members are on a course to change lives and institutions, and greatly enrich the culture of Los Angeles.

And *that* is truly amazing!

Carla Sands, President

FOR DONA KENDALL

whose personal vision,
generosity of spirit,
and determination
have helped build and sustain
the legacy of
the Blue Ribbon.

DOROTHY BUFFUM
CHANDLER ALWAYS
ADORED MUSIC

THE MUSIC CENTER
BEGINS

Dorothy Buffum Chandler always adored music. Her mother had been a music teacher, so music naturally filled the Buffum home. As a young girl, Miss Buffum played violin and piano, and then, as a Stanford coed, she sang in the chorus and light opera. When she was married to Norman Chandler, they bought their palatial house on Lorraine Boulevard in Los Angeles's prestigious Windsor Square; the couple decorated a formal music room with elaborate paneling and bought a Steinway grand piano, which some of the world's most famous musicians were invited to play. Nodding to modern-day enjoyment, the Chandlers' separate stereo room was filled wall-to-wall with classical music recordings.

Chandler's love of music motivated her to create something important for Los Angeles. Being married to the publisher of the *Los Angeles Times*, an heir to the Chandler family fortune, helped this enterprising woman climb to the forefront of civic life and achieve her goals. Paradoxically, her name would eventually become far more familiar to Angelenos than his. But throughout her marriage, Chandler was aware that being "the wife of" someone important

In 1958, Dorothy Buffum Chandler posed for famed Hollywood photographer Wallace Seawell in the music room of her family's mansion on Lorraine Boulevard in Windsor Square.

Music Director Alfred Wallenstein conducted the 1954 Los Angeles Philharmonic orchestra in the Philharmonic Auditorium, near downtown's Pershing Square.

gave her opportunities along with the burden of responsibility. She knew that the power of the Chandler name carried with it heavy expectations. But she also expressed an important personal need, one that was rather revolutionary in the existing social order of Los Angeles. "Once I took on a job, I had to prove I was not *just* Mrs. Norman Chandler," she said after the Music Center opened.

Known to intimates as Buff—never Dorothy and never *ever* Buffy, unless the speaker was totally unaware—she was the smart, athletic daughter of Charles Buffum, the mayor of Long Beach and the owner of the department-store chain that carried the family name. At Stanford University she was voted a campus beauty queen and met the ruggedly handsome Norman, son of Harry Chandler, who ran the *Times*—and Los Angeles—with an iron fist. They both dropped out and soon married. As a young mother to their children Camilla and Otis, Buff Chandler had no taste for typical female diversions like card games or women's garden clubs. Early on, she joined the women's auxiliary at Children's Hospital of Los Angeles, where she gave an indication of her future assertiveness and determination by toppling hospital protocol to fight for higher pay, regular days off, and sick leave for personnel.

Chandler also took more than a passing interest in what Norman did all day, to the point that, in 1944, he gave her an office next to his and her own job title—Assistant to the Publisher. To be treated with respect, she applied for a Social Security number and went on the *Times* payroll. She also enrolled in journalism classes at the University of Southern California, where Norman was a trustee. The newspaper's city room was off-limits to women, but Chandler was undaunted. She worked on a variety of projects, including writing Norman's speeches and working on the corporation's annual reports. In time, she focused her energy on reinventing the *Times*'s culture and society pages. In 1950, she introduced a way to pay homage to modern women involved in community service, women from all social strata, with the Times Women of the Year awards. The award was an unquestionable honor for its recipients, but also served as personal recognition from Chandler, who was involved in the selection process.

In 1951, her true philanthropic calling became apparent. The Hollywood Bowl, the Los Angeles Philharmonic's summer home "under the stars," was run-down and laden with debt. Actor Jean Hersholt, president of the Hollywood Bowl Association, asked Chandler, a regular Bowl-goer and a director of the Southern California Symphony Association, to join his beleaguered organization. Chandler sprang into action. She voted to shut down the amphitheater after its fifth performance of the season and headed a

"…this offer of donations of private funds to build public buildings is the most unusual I ever heard,"

said an astounded Los Angeles County Supervisor Frank G. Bonelli.

THE MUSIC CENTER
FOR THE PERFORMING ARTS

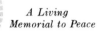

A Living
Memorial to Peace

Progress Report

Standing in the loggia of her home, Chandler and
financier S. Mark Taper reviewed architectural
plans for the Forum that would bear his name.

committee to launch a "Save the Bowl" campaign. Enlisting the aid of Philharmonic conductor Alfred Wallenstein, she scheduled two weeks of benefit concerts featuring top artists—including Jascha Heifetz and Gregor Piatigorsky—who agreed to perform without a fee. The resulting windfall allowed the amphitheater to reopen the same season. In the summer of 1952, picnicking inside the Bowl, be it in a private box or on a bench, was permitted for the first time, and Chandler has been credited by some with launching what became one of the beloved features of an evening at the Bowl. Whether or not she did conceive of dining alfresco, for Chandler's very first Bowl picnic, she enlisted Perino's, the white-glove, mid-Wilshire restaurant, to cater dinner and serve her guests.

The Philharmonic was founded in 1919 by William Andrews Clark Jr., a copper baron's son, attorney, and serious musician, who would occasionally join the orchestra on cello. He deeded his home, garden, and library to the University of California, Los Angeles, but his sudden demise in 1934 preempted any intentions he may have had to endow the symphony. A group of prominent citizens led by mining engineer and industrialist Harvey Mudd stepped in to create the Southern California Symphony Association to oversee its finances and management.

The orchestra was booked anywhere there was a place for people to assemble—from Thorne Hall at Occidental College to Pasadena Civic Auditorium to the Laguna Bowl. There were also regular radio broadcasts, including youth concerts at the Shrine Auditorium, and several performances in high school auditoriums each year, as well as summer programs at the Bowl. The rest of the time, the orchestra's primary venue was Philharmonic Auditorium, constructed in 1905 at the southwest corner of Fifth and Olive streets in downtown Los Angeles, a yawning hall managed by the Temple Baptist Church, which reserved it for religious services on Sundays. The lobby was cramped, there were poor backstage accommodations and bad acoustics, and the location was in a dodgy section of town across from Pershing Square. As it was, the stage was also shared by touring opera and ballet companies as well as the Los Angeles Civic Light Opera. The church banned artists and productions it found unsuitable.

For all its razzle-dazzle as a movie-and-television capital, its post-war housing boom, renowned centers of higher education, remarkable corporate growth, large swaths of an eventual latticework of freeways, and even several sophisticated restaurants, Los Angeles clearly still lacked a proper symphony hall. Adding to the city's reputation for cultural inadequacy, discussions about building an important new cultural center in Manhattan's Lincoln Square began in 1955, and formal plans to incorporate Lincoln Center for the Performing Arts were made a year later. In Los Angeles, the feeling of civic defeat was compounded when San Francisco's Cow Palace snared the Republican National Convention in 1956. At mid-century, L.A. suffered from a massive inferiority complex. One columnist of

Dorothy Chandler often took the stage at benefits; above, at the El Dorado party in 1955, and below, with then-Senator Richard Nixon in 1951.

Chandler was a masterful fundraiser who used every opportunity to ask, including this white-tie soiree; tiaras were not her style.

Buck Bags went everywhere dollars could be gathered—daytime or evening. OPPOSITE: Chandler celebrated the results with L.A. County Supervisors Kenneth Hahn, Warren Dorn, Frank Bonelli, and Ernest Debs.

$1.7 million came not from the wealthy and powerful but from ordinary lovers of the arts

who dropped their one-dollar bills into "Buck Bags."

the day described the city as an "intellectual and cultural Sahara." Of course, Dorothy Buffum Chandler was all for changing that—she just hadn't figured out how.

In the mid-1940s, thoughts of building a convention center-and-concert hall complex percolated throughout the city. America was in love with classical music—and Los Angeles was no exception. By the 1950s, the American Symphony Orchestra League counted 1,055 symphony orchestras across the country, up from fewer than a hundred in 1920; only ten existed in 1900. More than four hundred cities could claim municipal auditoriums, many with special music halls. With 135 million radio sets in use, broadcasting played an important role in upgrading American's musical taste. In 1958, Broadcast Music Inc. calculated that more than twenty-eight million Americans played musical instruments, double the number in 1936. By 1961, the *New York Times* reported that more Americans attended the symphony than baseball games.

Bond measures to build a home for the Los Angeles Philharmonic and a convention center were presented to voters twice in the early 1950s, and, twice, voters turned them down. In 1954, a third attempt failed. Chandler still believed a new building was possible, but she wanted nothing more to do with projects that were also bond issues. Once again, in another display of fundraising bravado, she set out to establish a "restricted reserve fund" for a future concert hall by holding an unusual kind of benefit at the Ambassador Hotel on St. Patrick's Day, March 17, 1955. "The Eldorado Party"—every detail of which was duly reported in the *Times*'s society pages—was so named because the raffle prize was a spanking-new, champagne-colored Cadillac Eldorado convertible, coaxed from General Motors by Grace Salvatori, the wife of industrialist Henry Salvatori and Chandler's ally on the symphony board. I. Magnin, the exclusive specialty store, presented a fashion show featuring the latest from Paris, including designs by Balenciaga, Balmain, Chanel, Givenchy, Madame Grès, and Christian Dior, who was commissioned to design a champagne-toned ball gown to match the car. Singer Dinah Shore appeared, comedian Jack Benny played the violin, and actor-singer-comedian and amateur conductor Danny Kaye led the Philharmonic, while composer John Green acted as master of ceremonies. The hotel generously donated the Embassy Room, as well as

The Dorothy Chandler Pavilion's Grand
Staircase glimmered on opening night.
OPPOSITE: Chandler's handpicked maestro
Zubin Mehta led the Philharmonic that evening.

the food and beverages. Raffle tickets sold for one dollar apiece, and the one-night windfall was a staggering four hundred thousand dollars.

The next month, the Los Angeles County Board of Supervisors appointed a citizen's advisory committee to find a solution to the convention center/concert hall dilemma at no cost to the public, and selected Chandler, by now a University of California regent, to run it. But after a suitable piece of land was identified, and the building costs were totaled, the price tag was an impossible fifty million dollars. Chandler was actually relieved that the dual-purpose concept failed, and the matter lay dormant for the next three years, with the Eldorado cache sitting in the bank. That's where things stood until Chandler impulsively set off on another course of action. She steered her bright red Mercedes convertible to Orange County and approached Myford Irvine, a member of the land-rich Orange County family, and returned home with a check for one hundred thousand dollars. Then she called on the Pasadena-based foundation of the late Michael J. Connell, who had made his fortune in a variety of ways including oil-and-gas development and banking, and secured an additional one hundred thousand dollars.

In January of 1959, Chandler told the symphony board, "I never experienced such a glowing fire of confidence as I do at this time, particularly in regard to a home for our great Los Angeles Philharmonic Orchestra. Through over a decade, thousands have planned, suffered, worked to bring this to reality. Now is the time to unite and build it." In March, on St. Patrick's Day—which she considered a lucky day—she presented the Board of Supervisors with an unprecedented offer: four million dollars in privately raised funds to build a symphony hall on seven-and-a-half acres across from Civic Center Mall on Bunker Hill. The land belonged to the county but had no intended purpose. "In my fifteen years in public office, this offer of donations of private funds to build public buildings is the most unusual I ever heard," said an astounded Los Angeles County Supervisor Frank G. Bonelli, chairman of the board. Chandler's pitch, the *Times* reported, won the unanimous support of the supervisors.

So began Chandler's real work of financing the building.

The price to erect a stately hall, then to be called Memorial Pavilion, on a spacious plaza with ample underground parking, was ten million dollars, of which county leaders agreed to be responsible for six million dollars. The goal was to raise the private funding by July 1, 1960. In the fall of 1959, the campaign kicked off with two Cornerstone Concerts at the Bowl, filled to capacity for the renowned pianist Van Cliburn, who contributed ten thousand dollars from his fee.

Chandler was now proceeding at a grand pace. She identified twenty-five thousand dollars—about four times the price of one of those Cadillac Eldorados, or double the cost of an average house—as an individual fundraising target, a donor level she called "Founder." Convincing would-be supporters to bestow that kind of gift required, she estimated, five successive meetings, not to mention consultations with her astrologer, Carroll Righter, the same chart-reader favored by many Hollywood stars and whom Chandler brought on as a regular *Times* columnist.

Sometimes, she would invite a prospective contributor to a formal dinner at home or at Perino's restaurant. Chandler always seated a possible patron, such as the head of a large business, at a place of

"Once I took on the job, I had to prove I was not *just* Mrs. Norman Chandler," she said after the Music Center opened.

Cary Grant and Nat King Cole
made it easy for her—
they personally delivered their
checks to her at home...

it happened to make wonderful photo ops.

honor by her side. "With Norman as publisher, she had their ears," said Lois Erburu, a frequent dinner guest whose husband, Robert, was chairman of the board and chief executive officer of Times Mirror Company, the *Times*'s parent company. "She would put a man next to her, and ask if he would like to help. She was comfortable around men. She was always a lady and handled herself beautifully. She was a master at it."

As further enticement for Founders, once the auditorium was complete, they would receive special courtesies including access to an elegant private room, the Founders Room, for dinner before a concert and cocktails during intermission. Each Founder would also be awarded name plaques on two seats in the front of the Orchestra level or in the so-called Founder's Circle that would be cantilevered over the Orchestra seating. A brochure prepared for potential Founders described a concert hall that would "at last enable Los Angeles, already endowed with all the other facilities of a great metropolis, to fulfill its manifest destiny as the cultural center of the western world."

Chandler created typewritten lists of likely donors—individuals, foundations, company heads—from Palm Springs to New York, and points beyond. In Paris, she had her sights on the famously tightfisted J. Paul Getty, and impulsively paid a visit to him at the Hotel George V, after which he came through with a twenty-five-thousand-dollar check. Following each name she made notes to herself such as, "already canceled and *refused*," no doubt referring to someone's blatant lack of interest. Or "ask Harry Volk to help," Volk being chairman of the Union Bank of California. Both Cary Grant and Nat King Cole made it easy for her—they personally delivered their checks to her at home, even if their generosity also happened to make wonderful photo ops for the *Times*.

Next to the names on the list, she also added the initials of whomever would make the ask, mostly her own. "Bing Crosby—DBC." "Walt Disney—DBC." "Mr. and Mrs. Alfred Bloomingdale—DBC." After the names of Jules Stein—a physician who co-founded the Music Corporation of America talent agency, which later purchased Universal Studios—and automotive executive Henry Ford II, she wrote, "DBC & GS"—"GS" being Grace Salvatori, who was named Times Woman of the Year soon after the Eldorado party. (In fact, Chandler also won Woman of the Year, in 1951, after rescuing the Bowl.) After Chandler, Salvatori "raised more money for the Music Center than anyone," Connie Wald, a top Beverly Hills hostess married to producer Jerry Wald, told Bob Colacello in *Ronnie & Nancy: Their Path to the White House 1911 to 1980*.

"Every day my mother was on the phone asking for twenty-five thousand dollars," said Salvatori's daughter Laurie Champion, who remembers coming home from school and being "shushed" by her mother, when she had a telephone receiver to her ear. "Mrs. Chandler always said

Architect Welton Becket designed every aspect of the Pavilion, including the gold-leafed fiberglass ceiling that floats above the orchestra, an "acoustical cloud."

Chandler would focus on 10 to looking at the whole list," she later

it like it was. She didn't beat around the bush. My mother was very, very gracious and very, very proper. Everything she said was perfectly stated and softly spoken. She'd couch it in such a way that everyone wanted to help, and everyone felt good about it. She saw Buff's vision, wanted to create something for the city, and realized they made a good team."

Chandler would focus on ten to fifteen prospects at a time. "If I had kept looking at the whole list," she later said, "I would never have slept." Her fundraising technique, she added, meant becoming "at various times a psychiatrist, a psychologist, a marriage counselor, and even a sort of family doctor. You have to know the family situation at all times. Divorce, illness, death—or just a routine change in the family financial situation—can inhibit contribution."

Chandler went after everyone with money, be they First Century Families—members of the organization composed of descendants of nineteenth-century Los Angelenos—or recent arrivals, particularly members of the Hollywood community whose newly minted wealth and glamour appealed to her. But this was no ordinary fundraising drive. Country clubs, law firms, and executive suites were all rigidly segregated along religious and racial lines; even actors were excluded from certain high-level social circles. The old guard, whose houses were mainly found on the city's "Eastside" (Pasadena, San Marino, and Hancock Park) and Hollywood newcomers, who gravitated toward the "western" reaches of Bel Air and Beverly Hills, simply didn't interact, unless they were college chums. In order to make the Music Center a reality, Chandler would have none of it and cut across the geographic, social, and religious fault lines. A half-century later, Harry Brant Chandler, her grandson, wrote in his book, *Dreamers in Dream City*, "In the segregated climate of the time, Dorothy soon realized that going to her blue-blood friends for donations was not enough. She had to bring together downtown's conservative establishment and the Westside liberal Jewish entertainment industry." But his grandmother took things another step forward—she also refused to hold meetings in private clubs with exclusionary policies. "I'm not like that," she stated. "I felt like the Music Center was going to be something to serve the entire community and not [just] the downtown establishment or the older families of Pasadena and here [Hancock Park]." In fact, Harry Chandler observed that building the Music Center did more to break down existing social barriers than anything else that had ever happened in Los Angeles.

Gordon Davidson, a young theater director whom Chandler would name artistic director of the Music Center's Center Theatre Group/Mark Taper Forum in 1966, has speculated that Chandler's progressive social stance moved collective attitudes even further along when she exhibited enormous tolerance for challenging artistic choices. "What she learned is that you can't separate what's on stage

15 prospects at a time. "If I kept said, "I would never have slept."

...she concluded
that Mehta was the
"right man, at the right time, right here."

from who's supporting it," said Davidson. "In other words, the bravery and the vision go together." In the book *Inventing L.A.: The Chandlers and Their Times*, former *Times* City Editor Bill Boyarsky went on to suggest that Chandler's open-mindedness "influenced the paper and became part of the evolution driven by [her son, publisher] Otis Chandler and carried out by his editors and reporters."

On weekends, Chandler spent hours at her family's mobile vacation-home on the beach in Dana Point, dictating thank-you notes for checks sent in, composing new letters of support, or—when checks arrived that she considered insufficient—brazenly asking for more. When Kirk Douglas contributed five thousand dollars, Chandler returned the money with a little note saying, "Dear Kirk, You could do better than that." (He did—bumping up to Founder level.) "Other people said, 'Oh, she did the same to me,'" recalled Kirk's wife Anne. "She knew that if you're thrown out the front door, you come in the back door. It wasn't, 'Would you mind contributing?' No, she would say, 'I expect you to participate.' There were no ifs, ands, or buts, and she got support from the people who were more or less running the town."

Even though word was out about Chandler's aggressive fundraising technique, her charm was considerable. "I don't think I had twenty-five thousand dollars," said Walter Mirisch, then vice-president in charge of production at the Mirisch Company, whose many hit films included *The Apartment*, *Some Like it Hot*, and *The Magnificent Seven*. Chandler may have been disappointed with his donation, but the two became close friends all the same. "She was very smart, had a great sense of humor, and I was very impressed with her drive," Mirisch said. Years later, she appointed him to the board of the Center Theatre Group (and later appointed him president) alongside Hollywood luminaries such as Rosalind Russell, George Cukor, and Lew Wasserman. "She told me she very much wanted to involve movie people in the Music Center project. She wanted those names connected with the place."

While she was forging ahead with her fundraising duties, Chandler's reputation took a serious blow. The esteemed Hungarian conductor Georg Solti had recently been signed to a three-year contract as music director of the Philharmonic. Considered one of the world's great maestros, he was planning to juggle an active European schedule while holding down the prestigious post in Los Angeles. For that reason, Solti, along with his manager Siegfried Hearst, proposed the name of the Bombay-born, twenty-four-year-old, up-and-comer Zubin Mehta to fill in for him. Mehta had received excellent notices in Europe and dazzled audiences when he made an appearance at the Bowl. But when the symphony board signed Mehta to a contract as assistant conductor, Solti claimed he hadn't been consulted first and insisted that Mehta's contract be canceled. When the board refused, Solti accused Chandler of trying to run his orchestra—and resigned.

Stories about Chandler's overbearing style spread like a Southern California wildfire. The *Los Angeles Examiner* quoted an anonymous member of one of her boards saying, "A meeting with

THIRTY-FIVE CENTS

DECEMBER 18, 1964

BUILDING THE PAVILIONS OF CULTURE

TIME

THE WEE[K]

LOS ANGELES'
BUFF CHANDLER

HENRY KOERNER

VOL. 84 NO. 25

(REG. U.S. PAT. OFF.)

Henry Koerner painted Buff's portrait for *Time*, so she joined an elite club that included John F. Kennedy.

Mrs. Chandler is like a meeting with Mr. Khrushchev; you sit around a table, and she makes the decisions." Another columnist chimed in, "The Philharmonic has been dominated for more than a decade by musically untrained, socially ambitious residents whose personal aspirations have overcome their professed sense of civic duty." The symphony board issued a statement defending her determination to build a permanent home for the orchestra and her desire to hire the finest music director in the world. Indeed, operating on instinct and with the counsel of Heifetz and Piatigorsky, among others, she concluded that Mehta was the "right man, at the right time, right here." She offered Mehta the position of the Philharmonic's permanent music director, an obvious "gamble," she conceded, given his youth and inexperience. But he was also a fellow Taurus (as was Gordon Davidson), and she knew they would get along famously.

In 1961, Chandler—by now a vice-president of Times Mirror Company—and her husband traveled to London, where theater-going filled their days. While overseas, Chandler realized that Los Angeles's performing arts center wouldn't be complete without a home for theatrical productions. "We must bring the theater into the center," she said upon her return. It's also possible that she didn't want Los Angeles overshadowed by New York's Lincoln Center, where the nearly completed Philharmonic Hall (which opened in 1962 and was later renamed Avery Fisher Hall) was going to be joined by two other venues that were already under construction, the New York State Theater (later renamed David H. Koch Theater) and the Metropolitan Opera House. In March of 1961, Chandler asked the Board of Supervisors to approve adding to the original plans by building two smaller structures on the plaza alongside the 3,200-seat Memorial Pavilion—an eight-hundred-seat Forum Theatre and a 1,800-seat Center Theatre. The entire complex was to be named "The Music Center, A Living Memorial to Peace."

With fundraising needs increasing, it was time to outfit "The Pub," the Chandlers' pool house on Lorraine, with folding chairs, tables, and filing cabinets. There, Chandler installed her Blue Ribbon Committee of women, each of whose sole obligation was to obtain a single thousand-dollar donation. Additionally, "Associate," another level of giving, was established. In return for a donation of five thousand dollars. Associates received a name plaque on one seat in the middle or rear Orchestra, along with Founders Room privileges. As for Dorothy and Norman Chandler's gift, *Time* magazine reported that the couple gave at least three hundred thousand dollars.

Construction on what was now called the Pavilion began in March of 1962. President and Mrs. John F. Kennedy endowed four seats. In November, S. Mark Taper, chairman of First Charter Financial Corporation, made a gift of one million dollars to the Forum Theatre. This was followed by yet another fundraising triumph: proceeds from Twentieth Century-Fox Film Corporation's *Cleopatra* premiere netted another million dollars.

The Music Center complex was dedicated on September 27, 1964, at a ceremony broadcast live on television and radio. The Los Angeles Philharmonic played its final season at Philharmonic Auditorium on November 20. In December, concertgoers mingled beneath colossal chandeliers in the stylish and spacious Grand Hall, and then filled the Pavilion to listen as the twenty-eight-year-old Mehta conducted the Philharmonic, joined by violinist Heifetz. At intermission, Piatigorsky turned to seatmate Jack Benny and said, "Aren't the acoustics wonderful?" Chandler and her husband watched from their seats in "The Hook," the protruding front row on the left side, facing the stage, of the second level Founder's Circle.

In 1965, the Ahmanson Foundation (initially funded by Dorothy and Howard F. Ahmanson, founder of Home Savings of America) gave $1.5 million to establish a special fund for the performing arts. The Board of Supervisors renamed the Music Center's three buildings: the Ahmanson Theatre, the Mark Taper Forum, and the Dorothy Chandler Pavilion, in honor of the woman who had pulled off the near-impossible by raising $18.7 million in all. Of that, $1.7 million came not from the wealthy and powerful, but from ordinary lovers of the arts who dropped their one-dollar bills into Buck Bags, yet another fundraising gambit dreamed up by Chandler and headed by Walt Disney, whose company designed and made the bags. Olive Behrendt, Chandler's close friend on the symphony board, was executive chairman of the Buck Bag Brigade. (Behrendt and her husband George, an insurance company executive, occupied The Hook seats on the right.) Taper gave an additional five hundred thousand dollars to the fundraising effort, bringing the total receipts of the Buck Bag campaign to $2.2 million. The Music Center's final fourteen million dollars of funding came from county mortgage revenue bonds.

Time put Dorothy Buffum Chandler on its cover, declaring her endeavor as "the most impressive display of virtuoso money raising and civic citizenship in the history of U.S. womanhood." David Halberstam, whose book, *The Powers That Be*, recounts the growth of the *Times* under Chandler's husband and her son Otis, commented, "If you're charting the coming of a big, sleepy, conservative community into the modern, affluent, increasingly sophisticated metropolis that exists today, she may be the single most important player."

Chandler, for her part, simply noted, "I've had very few days off since we started this." The hours and days and years she devoted to the Music Center serviced a belief deep inside of her. "There is just something within me that wants to make things more beautiful, serve young people, and create more opportunities," she said.

Yet, the hard work was far from over. Chandler realized that, in order to survive, the Music Center's resident performing arts companies would need a steady source of funding. As she said at the opening ceremonies, "These structures are no more than architectural vessels. Their significance—indeed their very reason for being—is determined entirely by what is presented on their stages…The Music Center buildings are completed. But the most challenging, the most exciting, perhaps the most difficult task—that of forging them into a truly great center of performing arts—has only now begun."

"The Music Center buildings are completed… the most difficult task— forging them into a truly great center of performing arts— has only now begun."

2

DOROTHY CHANDLER'S AMAZING IDEA

BLUE RIBBON
BEGINS

"A new Los Angeles '400' made its debut Wednesday at the hilltop home of Mrs. Simon Ramo," proclaimed the *Los Angeles Times* story. "This 400 will be composed of cultural, social, and civic women leaders in the Southland, and will be named the Blue Ribbon 400."

In mid-June, 1968, sixty-nine prominent Los Angeles women, from San Marino to Bel-Air, received Western Union telegrams with a cryptic message, "We extend this most cordial invitation for a program reception at the home of Mrs. Simon Ramo on Wednesday June 26 at 3 o'clock. An early response to Miss Burke at 625-1955 will be appreciated." It was signed: "Mrs. Norman Chandler, Mrs. Kirk Douglas, Mrs. Henry Salvatori."

Since the founder of the three-and-half-year old Music Center was involved, one could safely assume that the event had something to do with the city's new performing arts center. To be sure, regrets were not taken lightly. Marion Burke, Dorothy Chandler's longtime administrative assistant, was instructed to follow up and find out *why* a woman wasn't going to attend. And since Chandler held sway over the women's section of the *Times*, she never hesitated when it came to engaging the staff in promoting Music Center activities. Society Editor Maggie Savoy was briefed on the upcoming event over lunch at Perino's.

Libby Keck, left, and Grace Salvatori conferred at an early Blue Ribbon party. Another image from this event is on page 45. OVERLEAF: All eyes were on Gregory Peck as he spoke at the first meeting of the Blue Ribbon 400.

The response was less than auspicious. In all, twenty-seven showed up. So much for the famous Chandler clout. But the Blue Ribbon had to start somewhere, and Chandler knew she needed to rally her forces to move forward. Key players that day included hosts Virginia Ramo and her husband Simon, co-founder of the aerospace-and-defense behemoth TRW Corporation, who lived in an eye-popping, new house built on six acres in Trousdale Estates. The Ramos were important Music Center supporters— Virginia was vice-president of the board of the Founders, the organization for those who donated twenty-five thousand dollars, and Simon was vice-chairman of the Music Center board, eventually becoming chairman. For glamour, there was Gregory Peck, at his heartthrob best, representing Center Theatre Group, one of the Music Center's resident companies. For intellectual heft, there was Dr. Franklin Murphy, outgoing chancellor of UCLA and incoming chairman of the board and chief executive officer of Times Mirror. Erecting edifices was difficult, Murphy told the women, "but it is the easiest part of the

WESTERN UNION
TELEGRAM
W. P. MARSHALL, PRESIDENT

1206 (4-55)

NO. WDS.-CL. OF SVC.	PD. OR COLL.	CASH NO.	CHARGE TO THE ACCOUNT OF	TIME FILED
			THE TIMES MIRROR COMPANY	

Send the following message, subject to the terms on back hereof, which are hereby agreed to

JUNE 17, 1968

(Following message to be sent to the attached list of people)

WE EXTEND THIS MOST CORDIAL INVITATION FOR A PROGRAM RECEPTION

AT THE HOME OF MRS. SIMON RAMO ON WEDNESDAY, JUNE 26, AT 3 O'CLOCK,

1025 LOMA VISTA DRIVE, BEVERLY HILLS. AN EARLY RESPONSE TO

MISS BURKE AT 625-1955 WILL BE APPRECIATED.

MRS. NORMAN CHANDLER
MRS. KIRK DOUGLAS
MRS. HENRY SALVATORI

A telegram was Dorothy Chandler's preferred mode of communication. BELOW: Mrs. Byron Reynolds Jr., Maggie Wetzel, and Mrs. Richard Alden shared the excitement. OPPOSITE: A fine day for a kickoff with, from left, Virginia Ramo, Anne Douglas, and Mabel Fouch.

BRIEFING FROM MRS. CHANDLER
WITH BETTY BOSSERT AND EVE CRAIG, JUNE 25, 1968

The 6/26 Program Reception will be the 1st of a series of 4

The group will be called the Blue Ribbon 400

There will be no chairmen - never refer to the name "committee" and there
will be no meetings.

Those who are invited will join as charter members.

The 2 Presidents will be Mrs. Henry Salvatori and Mrs. Kirk Douglas
There will be 8 Vice Presidents from the membership

The 400 will be hostesses for social events, planning, Christmas play for
underprivileged

Each must be responsible for a minimum gift of $1,000 per year or more

Telegram will be sent in about 2 weeks for Program Reception at home of
Mrs. Chandler. Members will suggest to President names of others who
will fit in. Other names will be evaluated by membership committee.

Mrs. Salvatori and Mrs. Douglas will stay on the Steering Committee.
Need at least 6 strong women on Steering Committee

Next Progress Report will be devoted to the excitement of the Blue Ribbon 400.

Maggi Savoy attending meeting 6/26. After this Mrs. Chandler asking Joyce Haber.

Add to kits for 6/26 :

    Brochure
    Progress Report
    Pledge Card & Env.
    1 4 X 6 card to sign if wish to become Charter Member
    2 Memo sheets to suggest names of prospective members
    1 change of address card

About July 15th New Progress Report and Fact Sheet

"This 400 will be composed of cultural, social, and civic women leaders in the Southland, and will be named the Blue Ribbon 400."

–Los Angeles Times

creation of institutions. We have monumental buildings and technical resources, but we must come toward the twenty-first century with a commitment as to what will happen in those buildings." He added, "Build for your children as well as yourself; for the children of Watts and East Los Angeles as well as your grandchildren."

Always impeccably groomed, typically in custom-made dresses by Miss Stella and jewelry by Laykin et Cie, both from I. Magnin, the formidable Chandler let everyone finish their sandwiches and cakes and then stood before the fireplace to define her agenda. Clutching a strand of lucky turquoise beads "for when you have a big wish," given to her by a tribal chieftain during a recent African trip, Chandler told the assembled that she was putting together a women's group. She liked the name "Blue Ribbon" because it was the same one she gave to the women's committee who helped her obtain donors to build the Music Center, and "400" because that would be the cutoff point. Though she didn't mention it, the number also referred to society doyenne Caroline Astor's Four Hundred, a list of New York's elite compiled during the Gilded Age. Social cachet played a key role in Chandler's 400 as well. "Oh my dear, you couldn't just be anybody and get into Blue Ribbon," said Burke. "It had to be discussed."

The Blue Ribbon's function was to plan the Music Center's social, educational, and cultural activities and to provide financial support for the resident companies at the time—which, in addition to Center Theatre Group, were the Los Angeles Master Chorale and the Los Angeles Philharmonic Orchestra. But there was a huge elephant waiting to appear in the room that day. Even though the invitees were affluent, they weren't all happy to learn that the required annual Blue Ribbon contribution was going to be a thousand dollars per year. When comparable women's organization dues were in the neighborhood of twenty-five dollars to one hundred dollars, this sum was in a different stratosphere. Chandler had ruminated about the size of the donation. She consulted Joan Luther, a close friend who had a company specializing in social publicity. "I made the big statement of $250, thinking it was madness in those days, and she said a thousand dollars," recalled Luther. "She obviously had been thinking about this for a long time, years."

All but three of the guests attending that day signed their little pledge cards, so now the Blue Ribbon was off to a start, even if it was a slow one. "It seemed hopeless at first," said founding member

A Blue Ribbon event drew an enthusiastic group. OPPOSITE: Top, at home of Mr. and Mrs. Jules Stein, Mrs. Samuel Goldwyn, and Mrs. Hal Wallis, in '60s-chic dots, sipped tea, while a white-gloved Rosalind Russell Brisson joined Barbara Rush in the library. UCLA Chancellor Charles Young spoke with hostess Doris Stein, also in dots.

The following month, Doris Stein, married to Jules,

the Music Corporation of American founder,

opened her home to the women

for pianist Leonard Pennario.

"In Mrs. Chandler's mind
there are no hurdles, no obstacles
between an actor's wife
and an industrialist's wife."

—Anne Douglas

Anne Douglas, center, conversed with Anna Bing Arnold.
OPPOSITE: From left, Mrs. T. Brook Townsend II, Mrs. Long Ellis, and Mrs. Kellogg Spear (Camilla Chandler Frost) sipped wine at Otis Chandler's house.

Judy Murphy, Franklin's wife, of those early days. "Women just weren't interested in putting out a thousand dollars a year, and, after all, the whole enterprise was so new." Furthermore, Chandler didn't give a hoot if a woman's husband had already donated to the Music Center. She felt that women should be responsible for their own gifts.

Chandler needed help reaching beyond this little tea party, so she turned to two very different people, each with very different contacts. Chandler's choices of Anne Douglas and Grace Salvatori as Blue Ribbon co-presidents perfectly represented the constituencies she was seeking, and both could provide direct access to them. After all, who better to telephone Betty Wilson than her next door neighbor Salvatori? Wilson's husband William owned Web Wilson Oil Tools, an oil-drilling company (and would later be appointed the first U.S. Ambassador to the Vatican by Ronald Reagan). As for Douglas, being married to a movie star equipped her with one of the most golden phone books in Hollywood. "After a while I figured it out," mused Douglas of Chandler's modus operandi. "Mrs.

Another telegram announced an important meeting, this time in San Marino. Kirk Douglas, left, regaled Gordon Davidson and Olive Behrendt in the Trophy Room of big-game hunter Otis Chandler's house.

Chandler had thought of two women from practically opposite directions, and, at the time, from opposite political directions"—the Salvatoris being conservative Republicans and the Douglases, liberal Democrats. "In Mrs. Chandler's mind there are no hurdles, no obstacles between an actor's wife and an industrialist's wife."

It was really quite miraculous how the Blue Ribbon came together, especially considering the disconnect between social worlds. In those days, the town was divided, east and west of Perino's. The restaurant was, "the boundary line," said founding member Mickey Ziffren, whose husband Paul was a prominent entertainment attorney and a leader in the Democratic party.

"You used to think you needed a passport to go to Pasadena," said Ruth Jones, another founding member, whose husband Thomas was president of Northrop Corporation, the aerospace and defense giant. "In retrospect, it hit all of us—how did this marvelous woman have this idea to break all these barriers?"

"It brought the community together," said Alyce Williamson, Chandler's niece by marriage, and herself a First Century Family member. "I don't know of any other organization that has accomplished this."

Women remember feeling comfortable with the mix. "It was *fun*," recalled Jones. "I was thrilled to join." After all, the old social order was starting to feel antediluvian. "Culturally, (Chandler) helped connect West Los Angeles with downtown Los Angeles, two communities that (at the time) had almost nothing in common and barely spoke the same language," wrote David Halberstam. It was Chandler's "drive, energy, ambition and even hubris that connected them."

"The Blue Ribbon was an opportunity to cast a broader representation of leadership in the community," explained Gordon Davidson. "Without doubt, there was an idea of putting women in a position of power and giving them a voice. They may have started out 'blue' and 'coiffed,' but they became amazing supporters of bigger ideas as represented on the stages of the Music Center."

One month after the Ramo event, membership ticked up a bit. Forty-seven women gathered in The Pub, Chandler's pool house. As would happen again and again through the years, an esteemed artist was invited to appear—cellist Gregor Piatigorsky. In return for a member's support, Chandler wanted to impart information and culture, and backstage access to artists. She saw the Blue Ribbon operating on a different level than other organizations; there would be no meetings (other than for the board), no required duties—and no white-tie balls or even black-tie evenings for that matter. Any group could do that, and besides she and Norman just weren't fond of formal affairs. Not incidentally, word began to get around about the intriguing new organization.

The following month, Doris Stein, married to Jules, the Music Corporation of American founder, opened her home to the women for pianist Leonard Pennario. The newly named UCLA chancellor Dr. Charles Young provided encouragement. The Music Center, Young said, was creating a "vibrant, living, growing image" of Los Angeles, brought about by people not satisfied with beautiful buildings, but with providing a "rich cultural menu for all of Southern California."

There were more events, each one more exciting than the next. Zubin Mehta, Hume Cronyn, Elizabeth Ashley, and *Times* columnist Art Seidenbaum appeared together for a symposium moderated by University of Southern California music professor Dr. Raymond Kendall at the Salvatori residence. Libby Keck, who was married to Howard, the head of Superior Oil, welcomed the group for a reception honoring Carol Channing. Theiline McCone, whose

At a program about the city's performing arts, hostess Grace Salvatori (standing) joined, from left, actor Hume Cronyn, Blue Ribbon members Anne Douglas and Dorothy Chandler, Dr. William Melnitz, dean emeritus of theater arts at UCLA, and Dr. Raymond Kendall of the University of Southern California.

"They may have started out 'blue' and 'coiffed,' but they became amazing supporters of bigger ideas…"

—Gordon Davidson, artistic director
Center Theatre Group

Libby Keck, who was married to Howard, the head of Superior Oil, welcomed the group for a reception honoring Carol Channing.

husband John was an industrialist and former director of the CIA, hosted director George Cukor at her home.

"Very quickly there was a little bit of a snob appeal in becoming a member," recalled Anne Douglas. "It was like, 'Are you a member?' You knew that members had a little money, or they were all working hard to help Buff."

In time, the membership was composed of women whose surnames were immediately identifiable with business and power. Their first names were never identified in the roster unless the name was preceded by "Miss" (in ensuing years, that custom would change and women could choose how they wanted their names listed). Among the early Blue Ribbon members were (brackets indicate the member's husband's profession): Mrs. Harry W. (Virginia) Robinson [J.W. Robinson's department stores], Mrs. Alfred (Viola) Hart [City National Bank], Mrs. Earle (Marion) Jorgensen [steel executive], Mrs. William (Margaret) Pereira [architect], Mrs. Holmes (Virginia) Tuttle [automobile dealer], Mrs. Charles B. (Flora) Thornton [head of Litton Industries], Mrs. Edwin (Bobbi) Pauley [head of Pauley Petroleum], Mrs. Lew (Edie) Wasserman [head of Universal Studios], Mrs. Armand (Harriet) Deutsch [film producer; Sears, Roebuck & Co. heir], Mrs. Edward (Hannah) Carter [head of Carter Hawley Hale department stores], Mrs. John (Pilar) Wayne [actor], and Mrs. Bob (Dolores) Hope [entertainer], as well as Mrs. William French (Jean) Smith [Gibson, Dunn & Crutcher attorney], and Mrs. Justin (Jane) Dart [drugstores].

Judged on their own merits, nearly every one of them did what

Theiline McCone opened her home for a reception for director George Cukor. OPPOSITE: Libby Keck, foreground, hosted an event with Carol Channing, who's in the pantsuit standing between co-presidents Grace Salvatori, left, and Anne Douglas.

Ingrid Ohrbach greeted guests arriving at her home. OPPOSITE: The full-length William Draper portrait of Dorothy Chandler hangs in the Pavilion's Founders Room.

"She would say, 'I want you to do this,' and I'd say, 'I've never done that,' and she'd say, 'You'll learn,' and then you were dismissed."

most women of privilege did—they raised children, moved in a social world that corresponded with their husband's work, and volunteered their time. Some, like Blue-Ribbon-founding-member Olive Behrendt, transferred their training—hers as an operatic soprano—for a passionate support of the arts. "I just knew that, in our family, people did certain things to support the community," explained Marcia Wilson Hobbs, daughter of early-Blue-Ribbon-member Betty Wilson. Hobbs followed in her mother's footsteps and joined the organization two decades later. "What did my grandmother say?—'Much is expected of those to whom much is given.'"

Ultimately, many of those who signed on could claim a long and impressive list of philanthropic credits, some as board members and presidents of other organizations, some as major donors, some as both. Others would go on and found their own nonprofit organizations or donate buildings bearing their own names. Although they were born long before women moved into the professional world, they could all be considered "doers" in all senses of the word.

Douglas and Salvatori functioned mostly as figureheads and behind-the-scenes advisors to Chandler, without the complex responsibilities that presidents would later take on. They didn't visit the office daily or deal with workaday needs. Nevertheless, Chandler expected them to pull their weight. "She would say, 'I want you to do this,' and I'd say, 'I've never done that,' and she'd say, 'You'll learn,' and then you were dismissed," mused Douglas.

In time, as membership increased, Chandler saw that a full-time president was needed, and it was obvious who the right choice would be. The go-to person for Chandler, Douglas, and Salvatori was Helen Wolford, an intelligent and diligent woman who seemed capable of anything. "She was such a fantastic lady. You couldn't say no to her, either. Mrs. Salvatori and I were kind of the status symbols, and Helen was the working president," said Douglas. Within a year, 222 women committed as Blue Ribbon 400 members. As time went on, the co-presidents' term "just sort of disappeared," recalled Douglas. After Chandler and the team of Douglas and Salvatori got the group off the ground, Chandler made it official: Wolford was the first woman to be officially declared president and was ready to take the Blue Ribbon 400 into a new era.

THE CHILDREN'S FESTIVAL BECOMES A TRADITION

The 1970s were pivotal years for the Blue Ribbon 400. There was still resistance to join at the beginning of the decade. Frequently, a woman would say, "'Thank you, but no thank you,'" recalled Helen Wolford, the newly appointed president. "'I'm already overextended.' 'We can't possibly.' They could see no value in being a participant. They all had their own reasons—each person."

It wasn't until the mid-1970s, with fifty-three new women on board, when the membership actually reached the magic number, or 403 to be precise. The name was officially changed to the grander-sounding Amazing Blue Ribbon 400. Awareness spread by word of mouth about the unique quality of its events, through the high-profile women involved and by way of steady coverage in the *Times* society pages.

At the Music Center's tenth anniversary, honoree Dorothy Chandler signed autographs. "I love you all," she told the children. OVERLEAF: Welton Becket's glistening Pavilion chandeliers were aglow.

Mickey Ziffren addressed members, including the turbaned fashion designer LaVetta King, at a daytime meeting.

Special programs brought together Diane Disney Miller, above left, and Joni Smith; and Clare Boothe Luce, top left, and director George Cukor. OPPOSITE: In 1973, Blue Ribbon officers Martha Hyer Wallis, left, and Gloria Ahmanson met at Times Mirror Square.

Society editor Jody Jacobs reported on all the "coups," including welcoming First Lady Betty Ford as the guest of honor at a luncheon in the Pavilion, and listening to Secretary of State Henry Kissinger as he charmed the crowd at a "couples" event held at Times Mirror Square just down the hill. On a different front, one of Jacobs's columns began, "There was a day last week when the Bistro, I. Magnin, Saks, Giorgio, and the rest of the Beautiful People hangouts must have looked a little empty. The reason was that most of the best-dressed women in town were attending the Los Angeles Philharmonic Orchestra's rehearsal, another Amazing Blue Ribbon 400 event."

An extraordinary cross-section of women was arriving from different compass points and disparate social backgrounds.

…there was David Frost
moderating a dialogue with

Paul Newman, Joanne Woodward,
Jack Lemmon, Barbara Rush,

and choreographer Gower Champion.

"It could be someone from the movie industry the age of seventy or someone in Pasadena at the age of thirty…All at once, people began to be friends who would never have had the wildest reason of knowing one another," said Wolford.

For many, one of the added privileges of membership was being part of a powerful female network, albeit far from the emerging, glass-ceilinged world of women engaged in commercial business. Besides forming lifelong connections, Amazing Blue Ribbon 400 members received an education in a different type of professionalism—it was Management 101 in a roomful of ardent arts supporters, socialites, and power players, often all wrapped in one beautifully attired package. Although women had certainly worked together on charities before, the Blue Ribbon didn't bifurcate itself as many other charitable organizations did with a separate "junior" board. Here, the expectation was that young mothers would learn the ropes from women old enough to be their grandmothers. There was the synergy of youthful enthusiasm and old-guard wisdom.

Panels and special guests abounded, including a program on Shakespeare introduced by Adelaide Hixon, above, joined by Broadway producer Robert Fryer (standing). OPPOSITE: A bestselling-authors panel featured, from left, Charles Champlin, Garson Kanin, Jacqueline Susann, Bob Abernethy, Helen Gurley Brown and William Friedkin. Chatting with Brown afterwards were, from left, Suzanne Marx, Nancy Dinsmore, and Betty Rose.

Bob Abernethy leading a "bestsellers" discussion
with Garson Kanin,
Helen Gurley Brown,
Jacqueline Susann,
William Friedkin,
and *Times* film critic Charles Champlin

In 1975, First Lady Betty Ford held everyone's attention in the Grand Hall.

Pauline Phillips—"Dear Abby"—left, introduced Lucy Hubbard, standing, wife of USC president John Hubbard, at a discussion entitled Today's Woman. The Music Center's William Severns, top left, showed Wallis Annenberg Weingarten, center, Princess Alexandra and Sir Angus Ogilvy, right, a lithograph of Jacques Lipchitz's Plaza sculpture Peace on Earth.

Barbara Walters spoke at the home of Martha Wallis, who was married to producer Hal Wallis.

"I learned so much from these women," said founding member Lenore Greenberg. "They became role models. Whatever the situation, they were *ladies*. They never criticized people. There was a tremendous sense of decorum, and I found that so instructive."

When she was invited to become a member, Annette O'Malley was newly married to Los Angeles Dodgers President Peter O'Malley, whose company was a Founder of the Music Center. Arriving in Los Angeles as a "naïve girl" from Denmark, where she had designed costumes for the Royal Theatre of Copenhagen, she admitted that she found the group "terrifying" in the beginning. "I knew Mrs. Chandler because she was a big Dodger fan. I'd pick her up on the way to the games, so we had a lot of time to talk. She was incredibly warm and caring and funny. I was totally in awe of her." O'Malley was asked to join Blue Ribbon, but knew no one. "They were all very strong women and very different from the women I had known. Then, as I got to know them, I became very, very fond of them. It was a wonderful thing to happen for me. I learned how to get things done, how to be more efficient, how to work with other women. At home, most of my mother's friends would get together and drink tea in the afternoons. Support groups for the arts were non-existent. The whole idea of women getting together to get things done was something unknown to me."

Diane Disney Miller, an ardent Music Center-goer, also had ties to one of the city's most iconic companies as the daughter of Lillian and Walt Disney. At the time, her parents were Music Center Founders and the Walt Disney Company Foundation was also a Founder and a Benefactor (one hundred thousand-to-three hundred thousand dollar range); the Disney

Secretary of State Henry Kissinger charmed the crowd at a "couples" event held at Times Mirror Square

Dinah Shore, below, moderated a discussion with, from left, writer Neil Simon, actors Sidney Poitier, Charlton Heston, and the Forum's Gordon Davidson. BOTTOM LEFT: Dorothy Chandler and Henry Kissinger arrived for a panel discussion. BOTTOM RIGHT: Future-Los Angeles-Mayor James Hahn, left, and his father Supervisor Kenneth Hahn joined Helen Wolford at a Blue Ribbon event.

Maestro Carlo Maria Giulini struck a regal pose before the Dorothy Chandler Pavilion.

gift-giving would of course continue for decades. When Miller was invited to join Blue Ribbon, the thought that immediately crossed her mind was: "Oh my God, I've got to get some new clothes—they were all so well-dressed." Miller didn't know anyone in the group, either, but becoming a member changed her life. "I was with a group of women I wouldn't have known any other way. Their vitality and the strength of their connections, and their love of the arts" along with a common purpose, made a permanent impact on her, she said.

As for Wolford, she was a natural as the woman in charge—"one of those marvelous people who exudes leadership," according to *Times* social columnist Mary Lou Loper. But board meetings were conducted by Dorothy Chandler, who still kept a tight rein on everything to do with Blue Ribbon. Meetings typically took place in the Chandler home on Lorraine, in the library. Promptness was essential. Gatherings began at 10 a.m. on the dot and always ended before lunch. Nametags were unnecessary because Chandler expected everyone to know each other. No official bylaws existed.

Wolford put in full days at the Amazing Blue Ribbon 400 office located at the Music Center. As Wolford recalled, she and Chandler "were a team who spent eight hours a day, five days a week, figuring out how we could keep things moving." The two women talked constantly about what kind of stimulating event they could do next. They would look at the calendar, schedule four events per year, and as Wolford said, they would ask each other, "How can we give them something special so that they, too, will give something special to the Music Center?…Who are the people now that are of real interest in the world? Then you start with the unbelievable…I don't think Mrs. C. ever thought 'the impossible' couldn't be done." She employed a moniker frequently favored by people who weren't quite at the "Buff" level of intimacy.

Chandler offered Wolford her own tutorials in how to conduct business. Often, she would counter one of Wolford's suggestions by saying, "That's a good idea, but let's do it better than that." When Wolford told Chandler that she was waiting to hear back from someone, Chandler immediately asked, "Have you called him?" "I said, 'No, Mrs. C., I expect him to call me,'" Wolford replied. "She said, 'Dear, you can't expect him to call. Call him, and you keep after him, and *then* if you don't get any response, you call me.' She taught me to follow through constantly and

An Imperial mammoth fossil loomed above Harriet Deutsch, left, Gabriele Murdock, and George C. Page at his new, eponymous museum.

Members attended a private viewing of the *Treasures of Tutankhamun* at the Los Angeles County Museum of Art in 1978; OPPOSITE: Armand and Frances Hammer, top, joined the reception. King and Sylvia "Madame" Wu, with an unidentified woman, also viewed the boy-king's artifacts.

not to expect something to happen just because it's a good idea."

In rapid succession, the playwright Clare Booth Luce presented her "women's lib" play *Slam the Door Softly* and Barbara Walters spoke at the home of Martha Wallis, who was married to producer Hal Wallis. Stellar panels were ongoing—David Frost moderating a chat with actors Paul Newman, Joanne Woodward, Jack Lemmon, Barbara Rush, and choreographer Gower Champion; Bob Abernethy leading a "bestsellers" discussion with Garson Kanin, Helen Gurley Brown, Jacqueline Susann, William Friedkin, and *Times* film critic Charles Champlin; and singer/Blue Ribbon member Dinah Shore heading a conversation with playwright Neil Simon, actors Sidney Poitier and Charlton Heston, and the Taper's Gordon Davidson.

While raising her children, Wolford dove into charity work, and one of her favorite activities was creating arts programming for children across the city. She had launched a nursery school at All Saints' Church in Beverly Hills (after helping start a nursery school at Harvard Law School; when her husband Richard graduated from there, the family came to L.A. where he joined Gibson, Dunn & Crutcher), ran a children's theater program, along with the Art Council

It wasn't until the mid-1970s,
with fifty-three new women on board,
when the membership actually reached
the magic number,
or 403
to be precise.

Oscar-winning composer Henry Mancini and Nancy Livingston shared a Blue Ribbon table. OPPOSITE: A badge from the group's first incarnation; Terry Stanfill, left, and Helen Wolford attended a dressy event.

at UCLA, and was chairman of the thousand-strong Hollywood Bowl Volunteers. In the mid-1960s, she set out to disprove the theory that children and concerts didn't mix. The Hollywood Bowl had no interest in creating programming for children. "Everybody told me I might as well forget it," said Wolford. She persevered and secured permission from the Bowl management to hold a few weekday-morning family concerts during the summer. No one expected to sell anything close to five thousand tickets, but the first concert had an audience of ten thousand children and their parents. In 1969, Wolford's next step was to launch Open House at the Bowl, a summer festival for children with performances by a wide range of artists, both international and local, representing the wide-ranging ethnic community, followed by art workshops. The ever-popular festival continues today and is known as Summer Sounds.

Almost as soon as she became Blue Ribbon president, Wolford began envisioning a children's festival at the Music Center. The way to make a city grow and the way to make the Music Center evolve, she believed, was to involve youth. "Helen could see the big picture," said Joan Boyett, who followed Wolford as producer of the Bowl's Open Houses for children. "She was a visionary. She unified the Blue Ribbon women around something they could care about that would make them feel good. They always loved going to beautiful luncheons and beautiful homes, but they adopted the Children's Festival from the beginning."

In December of 1970 through January of 1971, the Blue Ribbon underwrote its first festival for fifth-grade children across Los Angeles, many of whom had never stepped onto the Music Center Plaza—or entered a live-performance theater. The experience of seeing world-class artists was provided to them at no cost. That year, there were twenty performances of *Story Theatre*, Paul Sills's Tony-Award-

Blue Ribbon 400

NEWSLETTER

SPRING 1975 NO. VI

The 10 Years That Changed Our World

A tenth-anniversary newsletter displayed a historic photo taken from the porch of a Victorian home that once stood opposite the Pavilion. OPPOSITE: Marion and Earle Jorgensen joined then-Governor Ronald Reagan and honorary Blue Ribbon-member Nancy Reagan at a formal tenth-anniversary celebration in the Dorothy Chandler Pavilion. TOP RIGHT: Judi and Gordon Davidson, left, enjoyed the festivities with Elsa and Ernest Fleischmann. BOTTOM RIGHT: Los Angeles Mayor Tom Bradley chatted with Gale Hayman and Fred Hayman.

winning play that came to the Music Center directly from Broadway, based on the fairy tales of the Brothers Grimm, incorporating improvisation and folk-rock music (Sills went on to form Chicago's renowned improv group, The Second City.). Blue Ribbon members served as hostesses to greet the children and guide them into the shows. For her determined effort, Wolford was named a *Times* Woman of the Year.

From the outset, the group's members became invested financially and emotionally. "The Children's Festival became the rallying project for Blue Ribbon," said Boyett. Many tallied their participation in the festival not in years, but in decades. "I worked every year forever," said O'Malley. Lois Erburu, who co-chaired the event with Miller one year, continued to welcome the children's buses for nearly forty years. "We all worked together and it was fun. You got to know people while blowing up balloons," said Erburu. "And we did it in our heels."

For the Music Center's tenth anniversary, ten thousand children attended performances in all three theaters, including James Levine conducting a rehearsal of the Philharmonic in the Dorothy Chandler Pavilion, the Aman Folk

For the Music Center's
tenth anniversary,
ten thousand children
attended performances
in all three theaters.

Helpers at the Festival included, from left, Mrs. Leonard Firestone, Mrs James Hoover, Hannah Pakula, and Maureen Kindel.

Ensemble musicians and dancers appearing on the Ahmanson stage, and the Mark Taper Forum's Improvisational Theater project. "Will we be invited next year for the Music Center's eleventh birthday?" one child asked a Blue Ribbon hostess. In 1976, the Blue Ribbon's biggest children's festival took place during the Bicentennial celebration. On each of five consecutive days, ten thousand children—fifty thousand in total—filled the theaters for performances and ended the day in a gigantic traditional American square-dance on the Plaza.

In 1978, the Blue Ribbon introduced the first Very Special Arts Festival for children with special needs featuring the legendary Emmett Kelly Jr. Circus, and that program became an annual feature of the Children's Festival thereafter. "Unless we give young children of all ages, all backgrounds, and all abilities the opportunity to experience the arts firsthand, this city will have no audiences and no need for theaters nor museums," said Dona Kendall, who chaired the event that year.

In 1976, Chandler retired from the *Times*. Much to her chagrin, the next year, the *Times* announced the Women of the Year honorees for the last time. Her son, Otis, put an end to the awards, wrote Dennis McDougal in *Privileged Son: Otis Chandler and the Rise and Fall of the L.A. Times*

"Unless we give young children
all abilities the opportunity to
this city will have no audiences and

said Dona Kendall, who

of all ages, all backgrounds, and
experience the arts firsthand,
no need for theaters nor museums,"
chaired the event that year.

A bookmark was a special souvenir for junior high school students who saw *Oliver!* in 1973. Baseball fan Dorothy Chandler attended a festival with Dodgers manager Tommy Lasorda. OPPOSITE: Supervisor Edmund Edelman presented a proclamation to Maggie Wetzel.

Dynasty. In 1979, Wolford decided to relinquish the post she had held for a decade. Upon her departure, she encouraged the Music Center to establish an education division to coordinate the Children's Festival with Los Angeles city, county, and parochial schools. The education division carried on Wolford's legacy with the Blue Ribbon's financial support—and womanpower. Boyett became the Music Center's vice-president of education. The division evolved to become one of the largest arts-education programs in the country.

That same year, Chandler turned to Blue Ribbon member Maggie Wetzel and—as was the protocol at the time—asked Wetzel to become the next president. Wetzel's husband Harry, president of the Garrett Corporation (later Allied Signal Companies), was president of the Music Center Performing Arts Council. As for Maggie, she was raising her children while earning a bachelor of arts degree in art history at the University of Southern California, and was ready for a break. She certainly wasn't keen on accepting a ten-year commitment. Chandler, however, wasn't going to take no for an answer. "She said, 'I need you so badly,'" Wetzel recalled. "I said I would take it for two years." Chandler upped the ante and set the precedent for all future presidential terms when she said, "Let's make it three."

"She said, 'I need you so badly,'" Wetzel recalled. "I said I would take it for two years."

Chandler upped the ante and set the precedent for all future presidential terms when she said, "Let's make it three."

POWERFUL
WOMEN UNITE
FOR THE ARTS

POWERFUL
UNITE FOR T

POWERFUL WO
UNITE FOR THE AR

A DECADE OF
CHANGE

By the 1980s, the Blue Ribbon had become a fixture on the Los Angeles social and cultural scene. The programs were varied: members watched a rehearsal of newly appointed Music Director Andre Previn leading the Philharmonic ("Blue Ribbon members were as quiet as mice," per the *Times* social coverage). Enrapt, they listened as General Director Peter Hemmings and opera-superstar Placido Domingo conversed as representatives of the Los Angeles Opera, the Music Center's new performing arts company.

In December of 1980, one month before Ronald Reagan's first presidential inauguration, the Blue Ribbon tossed an elegant send-off reception for him and his wife Nancy at the Times Mirror building downtown. Considered the Reagans' first official local social appearance since the election, it was a veritable society crush. An overflow crowd, seven hundred strong, was

Keith Kieschnick and Robert Fryer joined Carol Channing, right, at the Other Side of the Curtain. OVERLEAF: First Lady Nancy Reagan, second from left, was honored in 1983; pictured with, from left, Helen Wolford, Dorothy Chandler, Nancy Livingston, and Bettina Chandler.

When President Reagan walked onto the Mark Taper Forum stage during the question-and-answer session, Nancy was completely surprised, as were the delighted audience members.

Maggie Wetzel and David Murdock dressed in Western gear for a day at his horse ranch. OPPOSITE: In December of 1980, Otis Chandler and his mother Dorothy, both at left, welcomed President-elect and Mrs. Ronald Reagan at Times Mirror Square. OVERLEAF: In March of 1989, following the end of his second term, former President Reagan surprised wife Nancy, standing, when he stepped onstage with, from left, Marion Jorgensen, Joanne Kozberg, and Nancy Livingston.

"I knew every playwright
   in New York,
     and I had lived with a writer.
I wanted to not just show the
     product, but take members
behind the curtain."

–Nancy Livingston

a mix of not just Blue Ribbon members and their significant others, but a combination of Music Center and Times Mirror VIPs, and officials of the county and city, including Mayor Tom Bradley and his wife Ethel. Guests overflowed into the halls, but inside the Harry Chandler Auditorium, Otis Chandler, the vice-chairman of the Times Mirror board, took the stage with his mother, Dorothy, and Maggie Wetzel to introduce the First Couple. "I keep…calling him 'Governor,'" Otis said. You could call the event "California casual"—with the women wearing gowns (Mrs. Reagan's was designed by Adolfo; Dorothy Chandler's by Bill Blass) and men dressed in suits and ties.

The first lady appeared as a special guest at Blue Ribbon events two more times. She made herself available not only because she was an honorary board member, but because many of her friends, the wives of Reagan backers from the days when he was formulating his political career in California, were also members. Two years into his first term, the group hosted a luncheon in her honor in the Pavilion's Grand Hall, complete with a receiving line. When the president's second term ended, the group welcomed Nancy Reagan home again. Before lunch was served, she sat down for a question-and-answer session entitled Inside the White House. When President Reagan walked onto the Mark Taper Forum stage during the program, the first lady was completely

Andre Previn posed in thought.
ABOVE: Robert Joffrey and dancers.
OPPOSITE: Beverly Sills, left, and
Martin Bernheimer, with Nancy Livingston.

surprised, as were the delighted audience members.

The Blue Ribbon was evolving in fundamental ways. A major reason for the shift was that Dorothy Chandler's life had also changed. Now in her eighties, she was no longer working at the *Times.* Her husband Norman had died in 1973, and her best friend, Olive Behrendt—the other "tigress" (the colorful noun Denise Chandler, married to Chandler's grandson Harry, used to describe the pair)—died in 1987. Time had taken its inevitable toll, and the founder relinquished her daily involvement in the group.

"She would not have stepped back if she had still been in her prime," explained Blue Ribbon president Maggie Wetzel. But even though Chandler was no longer running meetings, the two women conversed a great deal about ensuring that the group would continue without its founder. Chandler strongly believed she had built a firm foundation and had faith that the Blue Ribbon would continue to build on it.

Britain's Prince Andrew and Sarah, Duchess of York were escorted by Keith Kieschnick.
OPPOSITE: Andre Previn was welcomed by, from left, Ingrid Mitchell, Corinna Smith, and Keith Kieschnick.

Kieschnick knew
what it took to get a job done.
She sensed that it was time for the Blue Ribbon to
"change as the city changes…"

Ginny Cushman didn't kiss the musician, but she did put her arm around
Los Angeles Philharmonic bass player Dennis Trembly during a "backstage
picnic." BELOW: Connie Wald, left, and Janet de Cordova attended the
Chanel gala in style. OPPOSITE: Nancy Vreeland met supermodel
Inès de La Fressange at the Chanel gala.

However, without Chandler's regular presence, and with Helen Wolford now living in Maui, decisions needed to be made about how to move the group forward, and Wetzel would set those changes in motion. Though she had Chandler's full support, Wetzel may have felt she needed to earn the respect of the group since she was an outsider in certain ways. "My mother grew up in Virginia, wasn't a debutante, and didn't live in Brentwood, Bel-Air, Beverly Hills, or Pasadena. She came into that scene," said her daughter Katie Murphy. Wetzel resided in Palos Verdes, hardly a backwater; but it was far enough away from downtown, both metaphorically and geographically, that she quickly replaced her "gas guzzler" with a VW diesel Rabbit for the commute to the Blue Ribbon office. (She and her husband still opted to fly to their vineyard, Alexander Valley, in Healdsburg.)

In order to proceed, Wetzel felt it was necessary to create a democratic leadership structure. For years, Chandler appointed presidents, co-presidents, and various vice-presidents. In fact, everyone on the board had a title of president of one kind or another. Under Wetzel, the board of directors became intrinsic to the operation of the group. She formed the typical committees that would be found at any nonprofit, including a nominating committee for new officers, an advisory committee to bring in ideas from the community and thoughts about restructuring the organization, a special events committee, and a membership committee. Wetzel also hired the first professional director to run the office. "It wasn't cut and dried. We went very slowly. We didn't want to change things too quickly," she said. During Wetzel's term, she also determined it was necessary to raise the members' financial commitment to $1,500, based on the needs of the resident companies. In response, fifteen women dropped out. Chandler, frankly, was not in favor of the increase. But Wetzel stood her ground, confident that the group was solid enough for members to withstand a larger financial obligation. Wetzel told Chandler, "We voted on that, and this is what we've done." Wetzel could not only stand up to Chandler, but she called her "Buff," a familiarity few members shared.

Wetzel's instincts were correct. Within six months of the increase, there was a waiting list to join Blue Ribbon. Indeed, by the middle of the decade, demand to join was so great that membership skyrocketed to 650. Accordingly, a name change followed, minus the descriptors "400"—for the obvious reason—and "Amazing"—perhaps because it was now apparent that the group's actions spoke far louder than the word. The new name was simply The Blue Ribbon.

By the time Wetzel's term ended, being tapped to become the next president was more than an honor; it was a tremendous responsibility. Each successor knew she had a large organization to run and even larger shoes to fill. "I was shocked," Nancy Livingston said when she was asked to take over the position. "Maggie was one of the smartest women I knew—and one of the nicest. She had a quality that everyone admired, respected, and wanted to be close to." Livingston tried to convince

In 1980, Joe and Beverly Mitchell, both at left, Jean Smith, and Walter Mirisch attended a Blue Ribbon members-only reception at Huntington Library.

Joni Smith, left, Ethel Bradley, center, and Joanne Kozberg were a well-turned-out threesome.

Wetzel to stay another year so she could follow along and learn the ropes, but to no avail.

Known professionally as Nancy Olson, Livingston had been under contract with Paramount Pictures, starred in several Disney movies, appeared on Broadway, and received an Academy Award nomination for Best Supporting Actress for her role in *Sunset Boulevard*. She became involved in the Music Center after she married Alan Livingston, a television and music industry force, a Music Center Founder, and member of the Music Center board of governors. However, Livingston said she felt unprepared to lead a large women's organization, so she accepted on one condition—that Wetzel remain as chair of the board. From then on, every Blue Ribbon president has moved into that top board position.

Previously married to librettist Alan Jay Lerner (*Gigi, My Fair Lady*), Livingston brought everything in her background in the arts to the job. "I felt there were a lot of teas for princesses and presidents' wives and vice-presidents' wives," she said. She observed that the focus on music and theater had somewhat fallen by the wayside. She said she asked herself, "What can I uniquely bring that perhaps a lot of other people can't?" She decided to design an event that explored the creative process through the eyes of the world's greatest performers. "I knew every playwright in New York, and I had lived with a writer. I wanted to not just show the product, but take members behind the curtain."

The result was the Blue Ribbon's signature series, the Other Side of the Curtain. Livingston launched it with Beverly Sills, director of the New York City Opera, and two members of the company. Also participating in the dialogue, at Sills's insistence, was *Times* chief music critic Martin Bernheimer. Sills, Livingston recalled, had a score to settle with him. Sills said that Bernheimer had a cavalier attitude toward opera. Sparks flew. After all, she may have been a diva, but he had just won a Pulitzer Prize. Subsequent Other Side of the Curtain programs in the series may have lacked the same heat, but always had substance. They explored dance with Robert Joffrey of the famed ballet company, music with the maestro Carlo Maria

Giulini and Ernest Fleischmann of the Los Angeles Philharmonic, and theater with Gordon Davidson and members of the Taper Repertory Company. For one event, musical theater luminaries Mary Martin and Carol Channing, starring together in the play *Legends,* shared the stage in a dialogue with the *Times'* Charles Champlin.

Livingston had other plans for the Children's Festival, as well. The Pavilion had become so fully booked that children were relegated to watching performances on the Plaza. But to Livingston, the performing arts meant more than a live act. She wanted to invite the children inside a glorious hall for the magical moment when a show is about to begin, and to learn the etiquette of being a theatergoer. "The lights start to dim, which is a signal to be quiet. The curtain goes up, and there's another experience," she said. To this day, the festival performances take place on the Dorothy Chandler stage, followed by dancing on the Plaza.

Keith Kieschnick was a relatively new Blue Ribbon member when she was chosen to follow Livingston as president in 1985. She had gotten to know her fellow members the same way most everyone else did—by rolling up her sleeves and pitching in. "I knew very few people," she recalled. "I became acquainted with them at the Children's Festival. When you come here and work all day, you definitely form new friendships."

She had a light touch when presiding over Blue Ribbon events. "I spent twenty thousand dollars today—mentally—on Adolfos," she joked, when the group was invited to see a collection of the New York fashion designer at Saks Fifth Avenue in Beverly Hills. A free spirit from Texas, she met her husband, William, president and chief executive officer of Atlantic Richfield Company, when she worked as his executive secretary. Kieschnick knew what it took to get a job done. She sensed that it was time for the Blue Ribbon to "change as the city changes," and set the goal of broadening its base to include young women and working women.

Music Center Performing Arts Council President Michael Newton, left, shared a festive moment with Paul and Mickey Ziffren.
OPPOSITE: Actor Henry Winkler sat beside Dorothy Chandler who celebrated her eightieth birthday at the Music Center.

She said the creation of Small Board lunches was her most significant contribution. Concerned that a membership of 650 made it difficult for people to connect, Kieschnick enlisted board members to host luncheons in their homes, events which took place every other year from then on. "Keith had a different perspective," said longtime board member Peggy Grauman, who joined the group in 1978. "She knew that the Small Board luncheons were important because they made people feel more welcome. That's one of the reasons I will end my days hosting them."

In June of 1988, several intimate luncheons took place on the same day all across town simultaneously celebrating two very special occasions: the end of Kieschnick's term as president, and the Blue Ribbon's twentieth anniversary. Kieschnick hosted one of the events at her home in Palos Verdes Estates. Anne Douglas, the first Blue Ribbon co-president, attended a gathering hosted by Erlenne Sprague. Douglas proudly reminded everyone of the goal of Blue Ribbon "to grow slowly and be a group of women who are really interested in doing things for the Music Center."

Chandler was unable to attend that day, so she sent handwritten scrolls, wrapped in blue grosgrain ribbon, which were distributed at dessert. They read, "Dear Blue Ribbon Friend, I am very happy to join with you in this way to celebrate our twentieth anniversary. We have certainly come far and accomplished great things for the Music Center. You mean so much to me. Thank you for your wonderful effort. Warmly, Buff."

Toward the end of the Eighties, a different type of woman emerged to take on new challenges for the group. Joanne Kozberg became the first Blue Ribbon president with bona fide leadership credentials, and her professional demeanor was impressive—she held sway with intelligence, calm, and decisiveness. Before being appointed president, she earned a Master of Arts degree in public policy from Occidental College and was a graduate of the Coro Fellowship Program, a training program for civic leaders. She also had the benefit of being a founding member, having joined nearly twenty years earlier, not long after graduating from University of California at Berkeley,

Wearing their official sashes, Marion Jorgensen, left, and Betty Wilson were poised for the arrival of fifth-graders at the 1980 Children's Festival. OPPOSITE: In 1983, Diane Disney Miller shared strategic plans for the Children's Festival.

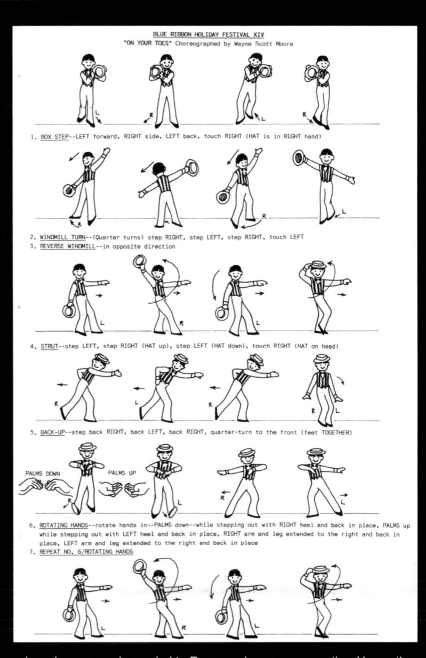

when she was newly married to Roger, an insurance executive. Her mother, Marian Corday, wife of prominent cardiologist Eliot Corday joined the same year. Olive Behrendt introduced them to the group. "She was my favorite of my parents' friends," said Kozberg. "She was like Auntie Mame. She said, 'Honey, you're joining.' I remember calling Roger and saying, 'Remember the couch you wanted to buy? I just donated that money to the Music Center."

During her term as Blue Ribbon president, Kozberg was appointed to the California Arts Council, serving as its chair and, later, executive director. Before and after her Blue Ribbon term, she worked in the government, first as a senior policy consultant to California Senator Pete Wilson, and later as Secretary of State and Consumer Services when Wilson was governor. In 1998, she began a twelve-year term as a University of California regent. In 1999, she was named president and chief operating officer of the Music Center.

In 1984, instructions helped classes learn a dance before they came to the Music Center. OPPOSITE: Thousands of children danced in unison on the Plaza during the 1988 festival.

The program from 1986 represented *Carnival of the Animals* by Saint-Saëns, featuring the Los Angeles Philharmonic. ABOVE: In 1981 one child drew a fitting "thank you" card; one of the costumed dancers, opposite, could have provided inspiration.

Yet, toward the end of her Blue Ribbon term, even Kozberg was unprepared for the snafu that occurred before a Blue Ribbon cocktail party at which she enlisted the newly sworn-in Governor Wilson and his wife Gayle as honorees. Catered by Chasen's and held at the Beverly Hills mansion of Barbara and Marvin Davis—a Blue Ribbon member and her Denver-oil-tycoon husband—it was an occasion no one wanted to miss. "The first day I got four hundred responses, and the Davises could only handle three hundred people. I had visions of everyone dropping out of Blue Ribbon," she remembered. "I ran to Keith and said, 'What do I do?'" Kieschnick told her to relax—a wait list for the Davis party would only create anticipation for the next exciting event.

Throughout her term, said Kozberg, "what always echoed in my head was something Mrs. Chandler instilled in us, which was that Blue Ribbon should provide opportunities and events that money couldn't buy." She brought Henry Kissinger back as a speaker and invited *Times* editor Shelby Coffey and KABC-radio host Michael Jackson to interview him. *Phantom of the Opera* star Michael Crawford appeared in conversation with Jackson as part of the Other Side of the Curtain series. Wendy Wasserstein, Pulitzer Prize-winning playwright of the smash hit *The Heidi Chronicles,* was the guest of honor at a new members tea.

With the resident company's financial needs continuing to grow, Kozberg raised dues to two thousand dollars, and froze membership at 650—which was as large as everyone believed the group could be to function and still retain its sense of camaraderie. Even so, there were fifty-two people on the waiting list. In 1990, she commissioned the first Blue Ribbon history to be written. And one of her primary initiatives was to provide tapes to schools to prepare children for their Children's Festival visits. "The children needed a context, and the teachers needed an ability to communicate what the children would be seeing—even if the teachers weren't comfortable with the arts," she said.

Kozberg also implemented additional directives for the board. She created an executive committee composed of all past presidents living in the area and some founding members, who would support the president and work through policy changes. The executive committee also would select future Blue Ribbon presidents. "Buff was very loose. She had the power of being Buff, but after that, we needed to set principles and guidelines," Kozberg explained.

Meanwhile, Children's Festival audiences were introduced, throughout the decade, to an electrifying array of performances, including the traditions of the dazzlingly-costumed dancers from Graciela Tapia's Ballet Folklorico Mexicano; to classical ballerinas performing to the music of Rachmaninoff by the Joffrey II Dancers; and to *The Bear That Wasn't,* Mark Taper Forum's Improvisational Theatre Project interpretation of the thought-provoking and amusing children's story.

However, with costs of putting on the Festival continuing to mount, additional support from members was crucial. Honorary board member Dona Kendall and her husband Dwight were among the first to step up with a significant gift. Starting in 1981, the Norris Foundation became an ongoing source of financial support. Harlyne Norris, the wife of Kenneth T. Norris, Jr., a philanthropist and former head of his family's Norris Industries, became a Blue Ribbon member in 1976 and volunteered to work at the Children's Festival as soon as she joined. An education major at UCLA, she was struck by the fact that not only had many of the children never attended a performance at the Music Center, but neither had a fair number of their teachers. "To see the wonderment on the children's faces—you can't put a price on it," said Norris, who added, "Hopefully, the festival plants a seed in them, and they'll want to return." As for Blue Ribbon members, both new and old, the Children's Festival would continue to have a deep hold on them, and its existence became a driving force for the organization.

MY FESTIVAL   MY MUSIC CENTER

1980

Prepared with their dance steps, fifth-grade students expressed joy as they danced in the Plaza during the Children's Festival in 1989.

Not only had many of the children
but neither had a fair number
wonderment on the children's faces
said Harlyne Norris, "Hopefully, the festival

never attended a performance,
of their teachers. "To see the
—you can't put a price on it,"
plants a seed in them, and they'll want to return."

In 1980, Annette O'Malley enjoyed a Festival
show right along with the grade school audience.

PROMISE
NGES THE 1990s
1990s PROMISE
E 1990 BIG CHANGES
CHANGES

BLUE RIBBON
LOOKS TO THE FUTURE

The Blue Ribbon commemorated its first quarter-century with a gala on May 21, 1993. The Beverly Hilton's Grand Ballroom was festooned with blue, beribboned banners that crisscrossed the room. Five-foot-high dogwood centerpieces adorned blue-plaid-draped tables, and desserts were individual boxes of chocolate mousse iced with delectable blue bows. It was a time to celebrate twenty-five years of financial commitment and service to the Music Center, along with friendship, always a key component to its members.

Bettina Chandler brought greetings from her mother-in-law Dorothy, the group's founder, who had celebrated her ninety-second birthday the week before. "I really feel Mrs. Chandler's presence here tonight," enthused Helen Wolford. "That lady made this city turn around. The Music Center would never have happened without her—and Norman. He supported everything she did and was so proud of her."

Placido Domingo led Blue Ribbon members across the Plaza. OVERLEAF: On December 10, 1992, Diane Disney Miller, right, and her sister Sharon Disney Lund, third from left, took part in the ground-breaking for Disney Hall with, from left, Deane Dana, Rita Walters, Ernest Fleischmann, Frederick Nicholas, James Thomas, Frank Gehry, and Edmund Edelman.

Hockney's colorful design for the Los Angeles Opera poster. In 1993, above right, from left, Lenore Greenberg, David Hockney, Sandra Ausman, John Cox, Nancy Livingston, and Peter Hemmings conversed at the Other Side of the Curtain. BELOW: From left, Constance Towers Gavin, Lenore Greenberg, and Joan Hotchkis made a chic luncheon trio. OPPOSITE: Chanel's Arie Kopelman hobnobbed with four glamorously gowned members, from left: Annette O'Malley, Sandra Ausman, Joan Hotchkis, and Anne Johnson.

"There were some misty reunion moments," reported Mary Lou Loper in the *Times* society pages. Indeed, the group's leadership was teary-eyed, particularly when all the past presidents—Maggie Wetzel, Nancy Livingston, Keith Kieschnick, and Joanne Kozberg—joined current president Sandra Ausman to pose for photographs. Founding members enjoying the evening included Flora Thornton, Violette Nason, and Ernestine Avery. "With Buffy behind it, I knew this group would be good," offered Marion Jorgensen.

The Norris Foundation was honored for its gifts over the years enabling five hundred thousand children to attend the Children's Festival. The evening also paid tribute to Iris Cantor, a Blue Ribbon member since 1984, and her husband, B. Gerald, founder and chairman of the board of Cantor Fitzgerald, for their financial commitment to the Music Center.

Sandra Ausman looked at Los Angeles from a unique vantage point. In 1985, she was appointed chief of protocol for Los Angeles County, a position created prior to the Los Angeles Olympics. When she was asked to head the Blue Ribbon six years later, she found that her day job gave her the confidence to run a large organization. Members of the Board of Supervisors naturally were respectful of her duties at the Blue Ribbon, since they were well aware of the group's key financial support for the county-owned Music Center (and aware, no doubt, that individual members were also important donors). Ausman joined

Blue Ribbon shortly after relocating from Pittsburgh when her husband Sheldon became managing partner of the Los Angeles office of the international accounting firm Arthur Andersen.

While helping out at the Children's Festival, Ausman remembered being impressed seeing the group's elder stateswomen, including Marion Jorgensen, arriving together in a limousine. Even though Jorgensen was a major Music Center supporter—a Founder with her husband Earle, and who together achieved Distinguished Patrons of the Arts status, that is, in the $250,000 to $500,000 category—she wanted to be at the festival for the same reason as everyone else: helping to direct children on the Plaza, get them on and off buses, and lead them into theaters.

Ausman said she paid close attention to Jorgensen and Jean Smith, who both served with her on the executive committee. "I watched how they made decisions. They had good business minds," she said of the two. Ausman recounted that when Jorgensen was serving on the board of the John F. Kennedy Center for the Performing Arts in Washington, D.C., she was asked "to found a group like that

At the Beverly Hills opening of Two Rodeo in 1990, from left, Joyce Hameetman, Joan Hotchkis, Jane Gosden, Maggie Russell, and Arletta Tronstein gathered to talk shops. OPPOSITE: Ballerinas with the visages of, from left, Keith Kieschnick, Nancy Livingston, and Maggie Wetzel adorned a window on the Two Rodeo mall, along with a *Zoot Suit*-ed Gordon Davidson.

"I met women who were interested in not just the cocoon of their life. They cared about the city. I wouldn't say we were feminists in any way, but we were interested in women making a difference." –Phyllis Hennigan

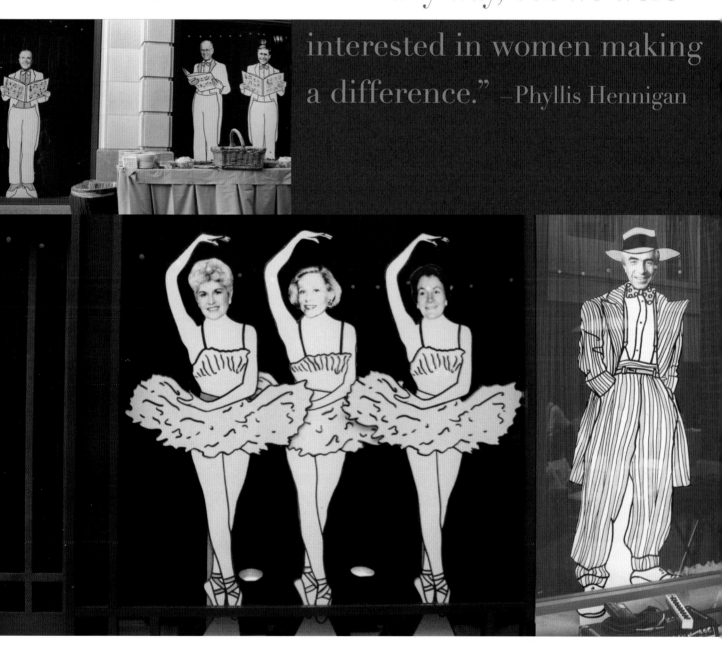

Phyllis Hennigan, far right, joined A. Scott Berg, left, Lauren Bacall, and Gordon Davidson at Between the Lines in 1994.

Nancy Livingston introduced Between the Lines, featuring a bestselling author—Dominick Dunne, and Blue Ribbon-member conversation with Pulitzer Prize-winning

Blue Ribbon in Los Angeles." According to Ausman, Jorgensen told the Kennedy Center board, "It can't be done! There's no Buff Chandler at this table. That was a moment in time."

There was no one who could argue that Chandler was the rare power player, and the proof was in the Blue Ribbon's strength during a serious fiscal challenge. When a severe economic downturn resulted in a sharp decrease in membership, the group never lost sight of its mission to sustain the Music Center. Membership settled at 450 women, still an impressive number by any standard.

Throughout the decade, the Other Side of the Curtain series brought forth intimate encounters with Music Center luminaries and visiting artists. In 1992, Esa-Pekka Salonen appeared first when he was newly appointed as the Philharmonic's music director and then, a second time a few years later, alongside director Peter Sellars. The Los Angeles Opera's Peter Hemmings and David Hockney discussed the artist's sets for *Die Frau Ohne Schatten*. Center Theatre Group's Gordon Davidson interviewed Jessica Tandy and Hume Cronyn. In 1992, there was also a private tour of the new Ronald Reagan Presidential Library in Simi Valley and another tour, led by Julie Nixon Eisenhower, of the Richard M. Nixon Library and Birthplace in Yorba Linda. Blue Ribbon presented an opening night event for Mikhail Baryshnikov and the White Oak Dance to benefit the Children's Festival and the American Foundation for AIDS Research (AmFAR). There were seminars to keep members abreast of new ideas in finance and health, along with fashion shows to appeal to their appreciation of style. In 1994, Nancy Livingston expanded the concept of the Other Side of the Curtain series by introducing Between the Lines, an occasional series featuring a bestselling author—such as Gore Vidal, Lauren Bacall, Dominick Dunne, and Blue Ribbon-member Judith Krantz— in conversation with Pulitzer Prize-winning author A. Scott Berg.

The Children's Festival continued to delight young audiences with its cultural cross-section of artists. One year, the Los Angeles Philharmonic performed a medley of American music—from Duke Ellington to Leonard Bernstein—while another year the Los Angeles Master Chorale, conducted by Paul Salamunovich, offered a patchwork of tunes—from the traditional Hispanic birthday song, "Las Mañanitas," to traditional American folk music. In 1994, the Mark Taper Forum's touring ensemble,

an occasional series
such as Gore Vidal, Lauren Bacall,
Judith Krantz—in
author A. Scott Berg.

Fifth-graders linked hands for their dance on the Plaza. BELOW: In 1991, newly elected California Governor Pete Wilson and his wife Gayle, center, were the guests of honor at a reception at the home of Barbara Davis (in pearls).

P.L.A.Y., presented a journey in *The Art of the Actor*, showcasing movement, vocal ranges, and lighting demonstrations.

And, the following year, on the occasion of the twenty-fifth Children's Festival, Helen Wolford was welcomed as a special guest at a celebratory luncheon. She burst into tears when an administrator from the Norwalk-La Mirada Unified School District recalled attending the first festival when she was a child living in Echo Park. All the past event chairs received proclamations from the County of Los Angeles.

When Phyllis Hennigan and her attorney husband Michael moved from Phoenix to Los Angeles, she immersed herself in volunteer work. By the time she was appointed Blue Ribbon president in 1994, she had already earned a seat on the board of Center Theatre Group. Hennigan made it a point to read through Dorothy Chandler's office papers so she could learn how to "fill those shoes." She viewed Chandler as a fundraiser to emulate, but the way the Blue Ribbon founder managed details also made an impression on the new president. Chandler personalized every note, always adding something in her distinctive blue ink, even if a letter was typewritten. Hennigan followed suit, and the notes added up. She estimates that she wrote some six hundred per year, thanking members for their contributions and additional donations, welcoming every new member, as well as personally inviting dignitaries, artists, and other leaders in the performing arts community to appear at events.

Hennigan once described the all-encompassing nature of running the Blue Ribbon. "I would venture to say the phone rings every three minutes. And when I get home, I have ten to twenty additional messages on my answering machine from people who don't think I really go to the office." She described meetings day after day, all across the city, from her own board of directors and executive committee, to the events committees, to meeting with the directors of resident companies, to personally meeting each prospective member. There was no substitute for being present, she learned.

On a larger scale, Hennigan began to master the art of negotiation. She learned how to work in partnership with the artistic directors of the resident companies, nailing down Children's Festival programming ("Ernest Fleischmann and Peter Hemmings—they were tough."). She also took her

Esa-Pekka Salonen became the Los Angeles Philharmonic's music director in 1992.

Clearly,
Blue Ribbon had become a

N̲ancy Thornton [Harahan], left, and Phyllis Hennigan helped organize the 1990 Children's Festival. OPPOSITE: California's First Lady Gayle Wilson danced with fifth-graders to celebrate the Children's Festival.

training ground for
Music Center leaders.

seat on the predominantly male Music Center board of governors, an automatic appointment for all Blue Ribbon presidents.

Hennigan observed that a new dynamic was taking shape within the Blue Ribbon. "I met women who were interested in not just the cocoon of their life. They cared about the city. I wouldn't say we were feminists in any way, but we were interested in women making a difference. Mrs. Chandler seemed to find the women of her generation who combined a social savoir faire with an understanding that you could, by being the wife of an important person, influence things in your community." By the 1990s, the social world was evolving as women were making strides in the world: the new philanthropic environment recognized each woman for her own authority and for her own personal accomplishments. The Blue Ribbon welcomed many new members who were presidents of their own companies, movie executives, scientists, doctors, lawyers, and other established leaders in the community.

When her term was over, Hennigan was appointed chairman of the Music Center Fund's annual campaign. Soon, she was president, and then chairman of the board, of the Center Theatre Group. Clearly, Blue Ribbon had become a training ground for Music Center leaders.

Appointed Blue Ribbon president in 1997, Joni Smith took a hard look at the group's financial picture. It was natural that Smith had her eye on the bottom line. She majored in business and finance as an undergraduate at the University of Southern California, and she was a partner with her husband Clark in their family-owned finance company. At the same time, her philanthropic resume was striking. She had been president of more than eighteen organizations including founding president of the Council of the Library Foundation of Los Angeles and founding chairman of its Literary Feasts fundraisers. She served on the Music Center's board of governors, before and after her Blue Ribbon presidency, for a total of twenty years, and its finance committee for a total of seventeen—and continued to serve on both boards.

In 1994, members were invited to see Walt Disney Concert Hall models in the studio of Frank Gehry, second from right. Among those attending were, from left: Music Center President Shelton G. Stanfill, Dona Kendall, Frederick Nicholas, and Sandra Ausman.

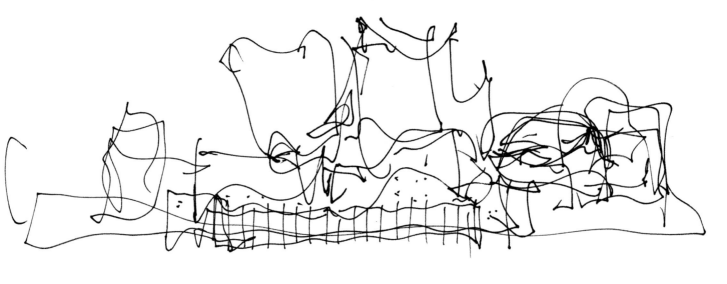

F. Gehry   Disney Hall   Oct '91.

When Frank Gehry's design for Walt Disney Concert Hall was finally a building under construction, its exterior spaces became an inspiration for a Blue Ribbon future.

When she was named president, Smith already had been a Blue Ribbon member since 1975 and had worked on the Children's Festival alongside Helen Wolford. Now, as president, she began to contemplate its future. Would there be enough money to continue this important event that meant so much to the children of Los Angeles? Its continually rising costs were more than members could offset with their annual dues, and Smith wasn't about to increase them. She faced the very real possibility that contributions from the Norris Foundation and large gifts from generous members wouldn't continue forever.

In 1998, with unanimous board support, Smith established a Blue Ribbon Children's Festival endowment. She determined that by raising three million dollars from members, Blue Ribbon would be able to continue the Festival in perpetuity. "People gave in all denominations and were wildly generous," she said. By mid-2013, the funds grew to $4.6 million, and there was an additional $1.3 million in planned gifts. Since its inception in 1998, spending from the endowment has totaled $2.255 million. "The Blue Ribbon endowment will go on forever," said Smith. "This is the centerpiece of what the Blue Ribbon is about."

Dorothy Chandler died at age ninety-six on July 6, 1997. Her ashes were scattered in the Pacific Ocean at Dana Strand. At the Dorothy Chandler Pavilion, the orchestra and the audience joined in a moment of silence to honor her. That same week, the summer season of Chandler's beloved Hollywood Bowl was in full swing. Two days after her death, the Philharmonic's executive director Ernest Fleischmann, whom Chandler had hired many years before, walked onto the stage. It was Fleischmann's last summer with the Philharmonic, but now he had the task of sharing the sad news with the crowd. He told the assembled: "The best way Dorothy Chandler can be addressed is by this great orchestra. That the Bowl exists to this day is because of her passion." He then asked the audience to stand for a silent tribute to the woman who had saved the Bowl almost fifty years before. After Fleischmann's remarks, Esa-Pekka Salonen raised his baton, and the Philharmonic orchestra played a piece he had long planned for the evening, Beethoven's *Egmont Overture*. Incredibly, it was the same opus Bruno Walter conducted on the night the Hollywood Bowl reopened in 1951.

6

BLUE RIBBON ARRIVED
WITH A PHYSICAL
BLUE RIBBON
ARRIVED WITH
A PHYSICAL PRESENCE
ARRIVED WITH
PHYSICAL PRESENCE

THE NEW
MILLENNIUM

A new millennium began with a new and unexpected project for the Blue Ribbon. It had nothing to do with the resident companies or inviting children to experience the arts. Instead, it was a way to bring attention to everything the members had accomplished. In the plainest terms, it was a naming opportunity. In an emotional sense, it was about women honoring women—and creating a beautiful space to do that.

In the early Oughts, Walt Disney Concert Hall—funded with an initial gift of fifty million dollars by Lillian Disney, a Blue Ribbon founding member, to honor her late husband Walt—began to take form across First Street from the Music Center. Disney's daughter Diane Disney Miller said that her mother spoke frequently with her close friend "Buff" about Chandler's dream for a new, modern home for the Los Angeles Philharmonic. Miller remembered saying to her mother, "Why don't you do something wonderful in Dad's name that you can get some pleasure out of?" When the project

Constance Gavin and the Music Center's Jeri Gaile featured Maxine Dunitz's book at the Children's Festival. OPPOSITE: Children ascend the stairs to observe the Philharmonic, a dancer *en pointe,* and the Master Chorale. OVERLEAF: *A Rose for Lilly* sits at the heart of the Blue Ribbon Garden.

A Journey
Through the
Music Center

This book is a gift from
Mrs. Maxine Dunitz

This book belongs to

dragged on for years, Miller heard Chandler tell her mother, "Lilly, hang on—it's going to be wonderful!"

As the construction progressed on the glorious Frank Gehry-designed structure, Music Center Board Chair Andrea Van de Kamp saw an opportunity emerging right before her eyes. She observed an open area with no designated function along the west side of the building that could be transformed into a garden—a beautiful spot that would not only express the "friendships and relationships nurtured at Blue Ribbon," but it would be a place to recognize the organization for its integral role at the Music Center since 1968. She proposed her idea to the Blue Ribbon, and through the work and support of the group, her vision became a reality.

In fact, Van de Kamp had been a Blue Ribbon member since 1979, after Dorothy Chandler personally recruited the then-associate dean of admissions at Occidental College. She had been living in Los Angeles for no more than a month when the two women bonded during a game at Dodger Stadium. The newcomer didn't even know who Chandler was, much less anything about the Music Center she built or her Blue Ribbon group. She was dating Los Angeles County District Attorney John Van de Kamp—her future husband and California's future attorney general. "I really want you to join," John later implored Andrea. "I can't alienate the *Los Angeles Times*."

Van de Kamp was a quick study in Los Angeles history. Fast forward to 2000 when she had risen to the top of the Music Center hierarchy as chair of the board and chief executive of the complex's fundraising and operations arm. She also spearheaded Disney Hall's fundraising campaign, along with civic leader, philanthropist, and SunAmerica Inc. chairman Eli Broad and Los Angeles Mayor Richard Riordan.

In an emotional sense, it was about women honoring women— and creating a beautiful space to do that.

Michael Ritchie, below, interviewed Cherry Jones on the set of *Doubt*. Andrea and John Van de Kamp, below left, and Music Center chairman John Emerson explored the newly renovated Griffith Observatory in 2007.

Joan Hotchkis was Blue Ribbon president when fundraising for the Blue Ribbon Garden was the major focus in 2002. She remembered a donation she and her husband John had made a decade earlier to Shakespeare's Globe Theatre in London. Donors could inscribe a flagstone set in the theater's piazza. The Hotchkises donated one in honor of their first granddaughter. Hotchkis liked the sentiment, so she suggested a similar fundraiser for the Garden, offering donors engraved pavers that would be set around the base of the fountain. She encouraged women to inscribe the tiles in their names or in the name of a woman they knew—mother, daughter, granddaughter. "It would be permanent, and it would be our legacy," said Hotchkis.

Disney Hall opened during Joyce Kresa's first year as president. The celebrations spanned a week. The three opening-night galas in October of 2003 were all chaired by Blue Ribbon founding-member Ginny Mancini—whose late husband, the Oscar-and-Grammy-winning composer, and his entire family are recognized by the grand Henry Mancini Family Staircase in the hall. Mancini said she hoped to create festivities that were "equal in excitement to the architecture and the music." As further testament to members' wide reach across the performing arts complex—and now, literally, across the street—the gala committee was drawn entirely from the Blue Ribbon's ranks—including founding members Helen Bing and Lenore Greenberg, past presidents Nancy Livingston, Joni Smith, and Joan Hotchkis, and members Carol Henry, Jennifer Diener, and Liane Weintraub.

Kresa oversaw the group's dedication luncheon for the Garden, which was held the week after the hall opened. "I was really new at all this. It was overwhelming," said Kresa. Yet, she knew that the day was perfect—and not just the postcard-worthy sunny, blue skies. It was perfect for all the members, including Diane Miller.

The centerpiece of the Garden is *A Rose for Lilly*, a stunning fountain designed by Gehry, inspired by Lillian's favorite flower and her collection of blue-and-white Delft china. A gift from Miller's seven children and thirteen grandchildren, the fountain is an open-petal design sheathed in a mosaic of eight thousand pieces of Royal Delft, imported from Holland. The tree-shaded space is reachable by public stairways on Grand Avenue and First Street.

"Everyone absolutely loved the Garden," Kresa said. "They thought, finally, the Blue Ribbon has arrived with a physical presence. To this day, when my husband and I go to a concert, we visit the Blue Ribbon Garden. I bought a paver with my name and one for my daughter and two granddaughters. They couldn't believe their Nana was president of this organization."

The Blue Ribbon Garden opening was spectacular in every way—yet it didn't overshadow other things that were happening. For instance, during her term as president, Joan Hotchkis had not only managed to oversee the Garden fundraising campaign, she also orchestrated the festivities for the thirtieth anniversary of the Blue Ribbon. She hosted the event at Rancho Los Alamitos, one of the region's original Spanish land-grant properties that had been owned by her husband's family and deeded to the City of Long Beach. On another occasion, the Hotchkises invited members for lunch at his family's Cojo Ranch, open land that stretches for miles of coastline near Santa Barbara.

Hotchkis also revived the biannual newsletter, last published three decades earlier, to keep members up-to-date with the latest information, and she established an annual luncheon for new members where they

Members had front row seats to an array of top musicians, from Bacharach to Domingo.

In 2013, Placido Domingo talked with L.A. Opera's Christopher Koelsch at the Other Side of the Curtain, and members explored the *Tosca* set, above. OPPOSITE: In 2011, Hal David, at microphone, celebrated his ninetieth birthday with Lionel Ritchie, left, Paul Williams, center, and Burt Bacharach. The tribute also featured Dionne Warwick.

could meet one another, exchange ideas, and learn more about Blue Ribbon. Always active at the Music Center, Hotchkis co-chaired Walt Disney Concert Hall's tenth-anniversary gala in September of 2013, with Blue Ribbon founding member Alyce Williamson, and David Bohnett, chair of the Philharmonic board.

"Joan Hotchkis was the best mentor I could have had," declared Kresa, when she took over the presidency in 2003. At my first board meeting, I couldn't come up with people's names or words I needed to use, and I just looked at Joan, and she filled in the blanks. I tend to be a perfectionist, and she helped me realize I was a human being, and that we can all laugh at ourselves. So that's how I went about things after that."

Kresa stepped into the president's role knowing she faced a steep learning curve. Other than serving as president of the Diadames of the Child Care League many years earlier, Kresa's days had always been filled with the obligations that went along with being married to the chief executive of Northrop Grumman Corporation, the global aerospace and defense company. Still, like presidents who preceded her, she was warm and welcoming and opened her home for various functions. "When Wallis Annenberg invited me to join, she gave me a list of board members, and I said, 'I'm sorry, I don't know anyone,'" recalled Kresa. Yet, Kresa and husband Kent's mutual passion for music helped her fit right in. Joyce had wanted to become an opera singer when she was young, and Kent's mother had been her voice teacher. Kent's father, who wrote music, was Irving Berlin's office manager; the couple dedicated the orchestra's backstage lounge at Disney Hall in the name of "Helmy Kresa, Arranger and Composer."

During Kresa's term, Nancy Livingston and Lenore Greenberg initiated the Sampler Series, allowing members to purchase a package of tickets to programs presented by each of the four resident companies. A few years later, Betsy Applebaum created a Junior Sampler Series so women could invite children or grandchildren to concerts and plays that were age-appropriate for them. Kresa also oversaw the formation of a Mentor Committee to pair established members with new ones to help them feel at ease the minute they walked into an event. "A lot of people wouldn't come to events because they didn't know anybody," said Judy Beckman, whom Kresa asked to head the committee. A Blue Ribbon member of more than thirty years, Beckman was also past chairman and board member emeritus of the Center Theatre Group. She said she believed it was vital to remove the Blue Ribbon's aura of exclusivity, so significant many years prior, and replace it with a new mantra of inclusiveness. "Our society has changed, and Blue Ribbon has changed," Beckman added.

For all Blue Ribbon members, the Children's Festival continued to be the essential annual event in the 2000s. It continued to delight thousands of young people from all parts of Los Angeles, who excitedly arrived in bright yellow school buses that parked in tight rows along an entire block of North Hope Street. The stages came alive with dancers from across the country—from the classical movements of American Ballet Theatre Studio and the contemporary movements of the Alvin Ailey II company, to the illusionistic contortions of Pilobolus, and the athleticism of Body Vox.

Honorary board member Maxine Dunitz wanted to find a way for children to enjoy their experience even more. Dunitz suggested that children should have something to take home after the festival, something more than a casual token—a souvenir of their visit. She considered candy, or perhaps a toy, but finally decided to provide an illustrated book that would impart information about the Music Center in an entertaining way. "Maxine had definite ideas about the book," recalled Kresa. "And she became a large force in my life. She showed me a determination for something she wanted fulfilled. I was grateful for that experience."

The first book, *A Journey Through the Music Center*, was given to each child for the first time at the 2004 festival. Inside are fun facts about the complex, a diagram of where the orchestra members sit, and a pop-up page showing the inside of Disney Hall. Vocabulary words helped the young readers understand the language of classical music, opera, dance, and theater. Dunitz also felt it was important that there be a space for children to inscribe their names, since many of them didn't have their own books at home. "This book belongs to:" is printed on the front cover. Because of Dunitz's funding, *A Journey Through the Music Center* would be updated annually. "It's such a joy and a pleasure," she said. "What can you say when eighteen thousand children at each festival say thank you?"

In all, more than eight hundred thousand fifth-graders have made their way to the Music Center

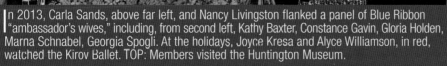

In 2013, Carla Sands, above far left, and Nancy Livingston flanked a panel of Blue Ribbon "ambassador's wives," including, from second left, Kathy Baxter, Constance Gavin, Gloria Holden, Marna Schnabel, Georgia Spogli. At the holidays, Joyce Kresa and Alyce Williamson, in red, watched the Kirov Ballet. TOP: Members visited the Huntington Museum.

Judith Krantz, left, Annette O'Malley, center, and Tricia Grey chatted before an event. OPPOSITE: James Conlon discussed Wagner's *Ring* cycle at the Other Side of the Curtain in 2010. Deborah Borda and Gustavo Dudamel conversed at the Other Side of the Curtain program in 2012.

during the Children's Festival, according to Suzy Boyett, program and events manager in the Music Center's Education Department—and Joan Boyett's daughter. The festival not only uplifts children and bonds Blue Ribbon members, but is a source of pride for the Music Center's own renowned artists. "Programs like the Blue Ribbon's Children's Festival instill the value of the arts and community, while helping children understand their full potential," said Gustavo Dudamel, the Philharmonic's music director.

In 2001, board member Eunice David and her husband Hal, the Grammy-and-Oscar-winning lyricist, put together an unprecedented fundraiser for the Children's Festival. They, director Walter Grauman and others produced "The Writer, The Singer, The Song"—an evening of entertainment with a star-packed lineup, including Dionne Warwick, Rosemary Clooney, and Helen Reddy. The Davids pulled out all the stops for three more of these sold-out shows throughout the decade. In 2011, the American Society of Composers, Authors, and Publishers (ASCAP) approached the Davids about producing a tribute to Hal in honor of his ninetieth birthday. The resulting event at the Mark Taper Forum, featuring musical stars Herb Alpert, Kristin Chenoweth, Hal's longtime-collaborator Burt Bacharach, and others, benefited the ASCAP Foundation education program and, thanks to the Davids, the Children's Festival, bringing the total windfall to the festival from all shows to five hundred thousand dollars.

Although all Blue Ribbon presidents never fit into one mold, Judith Krantz's profile was unlike the others. She occupied a place in the world far from the charity axis. At age fifty, she began turning out juicy, bestselling novels, including *Scruples* and *Princess Daisy*—ten in all, plus her autobiography. The *New York Times* once described her heroines as "smart, smart, smart," which could also be said of the author, who was always far more an intellect than her pop-culture status let on. Nancy Livingston and Judi Davidson, Krantz's book publicist—who is married to Center Theatre Group's Gordon Davidson—wanted to bring the writer into the fold, but being part of a women's organization was entirely new to her. Yet, after being consumed with her work, Krantz said she hadn't anticipated how quickly she bonded with so many members, like-minded women who cared about the arts. "When I moved to Los Angeles, I missed all the carpooling and joining things. I came here knowing no one. I had zero girlfriends. The best thing about Blue Ribbon was the friends I made. You made them through propinquity." She was quickly appointed to the board, hosted several luncheons at her home, and, in 2006, received a call from Joni Smith asking her to become president.

"I was so flattered, that I accepted, even though I didn't know anything about running a group," she said. As president, she applied her writing skills to the snappy profiles she contributed to the newsletter. And she made an unusual adjustment to board-meeting protocol when she requested that everyone stand and face the room when they spoke. "I'd say, 'I can't hear you.' So many people are reluctant to make their voices heard. If they only knew, it's their opportunity to have their thoughts projected." With costs continuing to mount for the performing arts companies, Krantz increased dues to $2,500.

She was proud of the wide range of events that took place during her term, such as the private viewing of John Constable paintings at the Huntington Library, Art Collections and Botanical Gardens. Founding member Lois

Alyce Williamson, left, and Marlene Billington guided the children to the Festival. Judy Beckman put her arms around fifth-graders. TOP: In 2006, Maxine Dunitz presented books to an excited group of children. OPPOSITE: Josh Groban beseeched Gov. Schwarzenegger to protect arts funding.

Erburu, whose husband Robert is chairman of the Huntington's Board of Trustees Emeriti, hosted a lunch in the Rose Garden Tea Room and brought roses for the tables fresh from her garden in Santa Barbara. The group also was invited inside the Getty Center's conservation department to watch specialists as they worked to preserve everything from classical antiquities to photographs. When Iris Cantor hosted an end-of-the-year tea at her Rodin-filled home in Bel-Air, it was another high point for Krantz—except for having to stand on a receiving line to greet all the members filing in. "It made me very glad I was never an ambassador's wife," she admitted.

Constance Towers Gavin did have experience on receiving lines, as she *was* an ambassador's wife— her husband John, himself an actor-turned-businessman and former Screen Actors Guild president, served as U.S. Ambassador to Mexico under President Ronald Reagan. Indeed, as the group's new president, this singer, actress, and musical-theater-leading-lady had a diplomatic style of her own.

Gavin believed that the Blue Ribbon's annual gifts to the resident companies, as well as to Music Center Education, could be turned into something beyond distributions on a ledger page. She wanted to create an event filled with meaning for both the givers and the receivers, a celebration where members could see where their contributions were going. In 2010, the first A Celebration of Support took place in Disney Hall's majestic BP Hall, where members proudly handed checks to representatives of each company. The program became an annual event and one of the high points of the year, where artists from resident companies perform and lunch is served in the Blue Ribbon Garden. "I can't tell you how much we appreciate this," Marc Stern, chairman of the board of Los Angeles Opera said upon receiving a check presented by Opera board member Alyce Williamson at the 2013 Celebration of Support. "The Blue Ribbon has been one of the most important and generous supporters throughout the history of Los Angeles Opera, Stern said, adding that the organization is the "glue that holds the whole complex— the Music Center and the resident companies—together."

Josh Groban spoke; kids listened; and the arts won hearts.

"These women understand the inherent value of the arts to society and have made the arts the focus of their philanthropy." —Deborah Borda

Jane Eisner, a past Blue Ribbon board member and a director of the Philharmonic presented the gift to Vicki McCluggage, another Philharmonic director—and Blue Ribbon board member. "We have so much cross-fertilization between the two organizations," Eisner noted, once again pointing to the many roles Blue Ribbon members play at the Music Center.

That cross-fertilization is the lifeblood for all parties. As Placido Domingo, the Opera's artistic director, said at a 2013 the Other Side of the Curtain program, at which he was warmly welcomed as the guest of honor: "With all of you we have had tremendous, tremendous support. You have made the growth of this company possible, making it one of the best in the United States and, for sure, the fastest-growing in the United States."

Appointed president in 2012, Carla Sands expressed that "overseeing a group whose cumulative, historic donations total seventy-one million dollars is the ultimate privilege." As soon as she took office, she said she relied on the leadership skills she gleaned as the eldest of seven children—and on the guidance of Blue Ribbon chairman Gavin. "For the first six months, I was glued to Connie's hip," said Sands. "She walked me through every question or problem I had. She is the most gracious person. It's not just because she is married to a diplomat. She has a lovely demeanor in running meetings, but a spine of steel."

A third generation doctor of chiropractic—who worked as an actress before returning to her practice—

The Master Chorale performed for A Celebration of Support in 2013. OPPOSITE: Eva Stern, left, and Pat Ryan co-chaired, and members lunched in the Blue Ribbon Garden, all as part of A Celebration of Support.

Sands remembered the day Gavin asked her to be the president. "I hesitated, but it was the highest honor for a woman in Los Angeles," recalled Sands, who was serving on the board of the Philharmonic at the time. "I'm passionate about the Music Center, and my husband and I are deeply embedded and involved." Her husband, Fred, a longtime Los Angeles Opera board member, founded Fred Sands Realtors. "The Blue Ribbon is the greatest group of women in Los Angeles. Our mission is clear. We work together well. We have fun together. When I present things to the Board I'm nervous about, or there are things that keep me up a at night, they'll be resoundingly reassuring—I know they are always behind me."

For any organization, contemplating the future is essential, and it is a high priority for Sands. "Let's look twenty years down the road. We need to ask ourselves, 'How do we sustain Blue Ribbon in the twenty-first century?' 'How do we keep the group interesting and relevant and dynamic?'" she asked. "It's essential, and we're up to the challenge."

One answer has been finding a way to address the demanding lives of the modern woman, whatever her position or stage in life. During Sands's presidency, Gavin and membership-committee chair Jill Baldauf initiated a program called Blue Ribbon Week, a time when members can introduce prospective members to the group. To accommodate women with varying schedules and myriad responsibilities, the committee designed a series of small gatherings held at different times of day—from morning coffee to cocktails—throughout different parts of the city. The success of the events in attracting a new and dynamic group of women proved that the spirit of giving remains at the heart of today's Blue Ribbon.

From its infancy in 1968, when a roomful of women stepped forward and lent their support to Los Angeles's grand new performing arts venue, the Blue Ribbon has evolved in numerous ways. Yet, with intelligent and determined leadership, the organization has remained as committed as ever to the values identified by Dorothy Chandler, who recognized that an organization of women can make a difference. And members continue to have a deep conviction that the arts have a powerful impact on the lives of all Angelenos, whether they are students, teachers, or longtime concertgoers. As conductor Gustavo Dudamel has said, "The arts are not just beautiful. They are vital to society."

Deborah Borda, the Philharmonic's president and chief executive officer, has acknowledged the philosophy that is central to Blue Ribbon: "These women understand the inherent value of the arts to society and have made the arts the focus of their philanthropy. Dorothy Chandler and Blue Ribbon members recognized that many years ago, and because of that legacy, we have a thriving Music Center in Los Angeles."

And so, the power of one woman's vision to enrich the lives of so many will continue year after year after year.

And so,

the power of one woman's vision

to enrich the lives of so many

will continue

year after year

after year.

The Blue Ribbon Membership
June 1968–August 2013

This list was created using many accounting, Music Center, and Blue Ribbon records. Because this is a historical document, to the best of our ability we have listed each member as she initially requested to be listed when she joined The Blue Ribbon. We have included first names in parentheses to help identify members. When known, we have also included a member's revised name in square brackets if she changed it since first joining. Members who left Blue Ribbon for a period and later rejoined are listed by the initial date of their membership.

This is a living document. We apologize for any mistakes. If you have an update or edit to the list, we welcome your changes. Please contact The Blue Ribbon Office at the Music Center.

Joined in 1968:

Mrs. Walter H. Annenberg (Lee)
Mrs. Aerol Arnold (Anna Bing)
Mrs. Waldo A. Avery (Alice)
Mrs. R. Stanton Avery (Ernestine)
Mrs. MacDonald Becket (Marjorie)
Mrs. George S. Behrendt (Olive)
Mrs. Jack Benny (Mary)
Mrs. Edgar Bergen (Frances)
Mrs. Marshall Berges (Mildred)
Mrs. Andrew D. Berkey II (Jackie)
Mrs. William J. Bettingen (Burton)
Mrs. Peter S. Bing (Helen)
Mrs. Franklin Otis Booth Jr. [Mrs. John Waugh] (Dody)
Mrs. Samuel F. Bowlby (Billie)
Mrs. E. John Brandeis (Marjorie)
Mrs. Samuel J. Briskin (Sara)
Mrs. George C. Brock (Margaret)
Mrs. Willard Everett Brown (Dorothy)
Mrs. Douglas B. Brown (Susan)
Mrs. Shirley C. Burden (Julie)
Mrs. William Henry Burgess (Clara)
Mrs. Albert V. Casey (Eleanor)
Mrs. Norman Chandler (Dorothy Buffum)
Mrs. Ralph J. Chandler (Lenore)
Mrs. John Wreford Chapple (Meg)
Mrs. Nicholas Chapro (Fania)
Mrs. Frank Clark Jr. (Dorothy)
Mrs. Thurmond Clarke (Athalie)
Mrs. William B. Coberly (Vicki)
Mrs. Whitley C. Collins (Amelia)
Mrs. John Connell (Carol)
Mrs. John Brown Cook (Marian)
Mrs. Eliot Corday (Marian)
Mrs. Homer D. Crotty (Ida)
Mrs. Warren H. Crowell (Dorothy)
Mrs. Elliot Cummings (Mary)
Mrs. Justin Dart (Jane)
Mrs. W. Thomas Davis (Elizabeth)
Mrs. Mark Justin Dees (Eleanor)
Mrs. Armand S. Deutsch (Harriet)
Mrs. Brad Dexter (Mary)
Mrs. Walt Disney (Lillian)
Mrs. Kirk Douglas (Anne)
Mrs. Henry Dreyfuss (Doris)
Mrs. William W. Durney (Dorothy)
Mrs. Hugh H. Evans (Gladys)
Mrs. William E. Forbes (Ann)
Mrs. Theodore A. Fouch (Mabel)
Mrs. Samuel Goldwyn (Frances)

Mrs. Stafford R. Grady (Roberta)
Mrs. John W. Green (Bonnie)
Mrs. Dorothy Green
Mrs. Z. Wayne Griffin (Elinor)
Mrs. Antoinette Zellerbach Haber (Tony)
Mrs. Louis M. Halper (Birdie)
Mrs. Robert A. Hamilton (Florence)
Mrs. Chauncey J. Hamlin Jr.
Mrs. Armand Hammer (Frances)
Mrs. John W. Hancock II (Margaret)
Mrs. Edwin L. Harbach (Allie)
Mrs. Alfred Hart (Viola)
Mrs. Morton A. Heller (Lita)
Mrs. Henry L. Hilty (Christine)
Mrs. Hart Isaacs Jr. (Patricia)
Mrs. Sinclair Jardine (Ann)
Mrs. Kenneth S. Jeffrey (Marie)
Mrs. Luther H. Johnson (Rita)
Mrs. Thomas V. Jones (Ruth)
Mrs. Earle M. Jorgensen (Marion)
Mrs. Danny Kaye (Sylvia)
Mrs. Lewis A. Kingsley [Mrs. Richard Elkus] (Merle)
Mrs. Frederick C. Kingston (Virginia)
Mrs. Gladys Q. Knapp
Mrs. Joseph B. Koepfli (Ann)
Mrs. Roger A. Kozberg (Joanne)
Mrs. Warren Francis Lamb (Ruby)
Mrs. Frederick G. Larkin Jr. (Fran)
Mrs. Mervyn Leroy (Kitty)
Mrs. Joseph L. Levy (Bessie)
Mrs. Milton Lewis (Lollie)
Mrs. Charles A. Luckman (Harriet)
Mrs. Charles W. Luther (Joan)
Mrs. Roy C. Markus (Eva)
Miss Patricia A. Martin
Mrs. Tom May (Anita)
Mrs. John Alex McCone (Ty)
Mrs. Giles W. Mead (Elise)
Mrs. Glen H. Mitchel Jr.
Mrs. John E. Mock (Jane)
Mrs. Victor Montgomery Sr. (Gladys)
Mrs. Hughes Gregory Morton (Mary)
Mrs. Lindley C. Morton (Ruth)
Mrs. Franklin D. Murphy (Judy)
Mrs. Fred Nason Sr. (Vi)
Mrs. Michael Nidorf (Lorena)
Mrs. Kenneth T. Norris (Eileen)
Mrs. Anthony Owen (Donna)
Mrs. William Pagen (Barbara)
Mrs. Leona Palmer
Mrs. Arthur L. Park Jr. (Merrill)

Mrs. Vidor Parry (Suzanne)
Mrs. Kenneth M. Payne (Lina)
Mrs. Clair L. Peck Jr. (Emily)
Mrs. Gregory Peck (Veronique)
Mrs. William L. Pereira (Margaret)
Mrs. Edwin S. Phillips (Joan)
Mrs. Spiros G. Ponty (Tina)
Mrs. Irving Prell (Evelyn)
Mrs. Simon Ramo (Virginia)
Mrs. John A. Richards (Carol)
Mrs. Harry W. Robinson (Virginia)
Mrs. Sydney J. Rosenberg (Jackie)
Mrs. H. Palmer Sabin (Dorothea)
Mrs. Henry Salvatori (Grace)
Mrs. Eric Scudder (Marie)
Mrs. George Seaton (Phyllis)
Dr. Lillian P. Seitsive
Mrs. Lucille Ellis Simon
Mrs. Nancy Sinatra
Mrs. H. Russell Smith (Jeanne)
Mrs. Norman F. Sprague Jr. (Caryll)
Mrs. Harold M. Stern (Marion)
Mrs. James D. Stewart (Elaine)
Mrs. Larry Superstein (Leah)
Mrs. John Swope (Dorothy)
Mrs. Charles B. Thornton (Flora)
Mrs. Nina B. Trutanic
Mrs. Arch Rollin Tuthill (Helen)
Mrs. John C. Tyler (Alice)
Mrs. Hal B. Wallis (Martha)
Mrs. Lew R. Wasserman (Edith)
Mrs. Martin Weil (Dixie)
Mrs. Seth Weingarten [Ms. Wallis Annenberg]
Mrs. Marcia S. Weisman
Mrs. Maurice M. Weiss (Edna)
Mrs. Charles A. Wellman (Lela)
Mrs. Dwight Whiting (Ethel)
Mrs. Donald Witherbee (Tory)
Mrs. William Witherspoon (Gertrude)
Mrs. Jack D. Wrather Jr. (Bunny)
Mrs. Abe M. Zarem (Esther)
Mrs. Paul Ziffren (Mickey)

Joined in 1969:

Mrs. Howard F. Ahmanson (Caroline)
Mrs. William H. Ahmanson (Gloria)
Mrs. Robert H. Ahmanson (Kathy)
Mrs. Hoxie Anderson (Alice)
Mrs. Roy L. Ash (Lila)
Mrs. Norman Barker Jr. (Sue)
Mrs. Ross Beason

Mrs. George Bjurman (Dorothy)
Mrs. Alfred Bloomingdale (Betsy)
Mrs. Robert F. Blumofe (Joan)
Mrs. John Bowles (Norma)
Mrs. John Gilbert Braun (Ruth)
Mrs. Frederick Brisson (Rosalind Russell)
Mrs. Harold C. Brooks
Mrs. John G. Brooks
Mrs. Robert S. Burns
Mrs. James Y. Camp
Mrs. Walter W. Candy Jr. (Sit)
Mrs. Victor M. Carter (Adrea)
Mrs. Edward William Carter (Hannah)
Mrs. Otis Chandler [Mrs. Patrick De Young] (Missy)
Mrs. Myron T. Chapro
Mrs. George Chasin (Eileen)
Mrs. Leonard Chudacoff Sr. (Rose)
Mrs. William Clayton (Fran)
Mrs. Mario Clinco
Mrs. William H. Coleman (Isabel)
Mrs. Harold P. Cooper (Marta)
Mrs. Clark Cornell
Mrs. Robert W. Craig (Eve)
Mrs. Gordon B. Crary
Mrs. Theodore E. Cummings (Sue)
Mrs. Robert Cummings
Mrs. James Curley (Marcia)
Mrs. Robert M. Daiss (Jane)
Mrs. Mary B. de Long
Mrs. Henry de Roulet (Dawnie)
Mrs. Henry O. Duque (Elizabeth)
Mrs. Anthony Duquette (Beagle)
Mrs. Rollin Pollard Eckis (Caroline)
Mrs. Henry O. Eversole Jr.
Mrs. Gary R. Familian (Elisabeth Adler)
Mrs. Freddie Fields (Polly Bergen)
Mrs. Leonard Firestone (Nicky)
Mrs. John Simon Fluor (Marjorie)
Mrs. Edward T. Foley (Jean)
Mrs. William R. Forman (Dorothy)
Mrs. F. Daniel Frost (Margie)
Mrs. Kennedy B. Galpin (Bobby)
Mrs. George F. Getty II (Jackie)
Mrs. Richard E. Gold (Harriet)
Mrs. Charles I. Gold (Ruth)
Mrs. Bernard A. Greenberg (Lenore)
Mrs. Robert Frank Gross
Mrs. B. Joseph Hammond (Bea)
Mrs. Charles Haubiel (Mary)
Mrs. Joseph H. Hazen (Lita)

Mrs. Royce H. Heath (Fern)
Mrs. Richard H. Hellman (Dotsy)
Mrs. Robert D. Hillman (Barbara)
Mrs. Alexander P. Hixon (Adelaide)
Mrs. Bob Hope (Dolores)
Mrs. J.L. Hurschler (Flora)
Mrs. Deane F. Johnson (Anne)
Mrs. Gerald Kales
Mrs. Eugene V. Klein (Joyce)
Mrs. Erich Koenig (Della)
Mrs. Albert F. Leland
Mrs. Harry Lenart (Yvonne)
Mrs. Harry Lewis (Marilyn)
Mrs. Bert Burgess Malouf (Marion)
Mrs. Henry Mancini (Ginny)
Mrs. Walter N. Marks (Doris)
Mrs. David May II (Dee)
Mrs. Clifford May (Lisa)
Mrs. Robert B. McLain (Josephine Holmes)
Mrs. Owens Miller (Margaret Mary)
Mrs. Joseph N. Mitchell (Beverly)
Mrs. Nebeker Mudd
Mrs. Daniel Nadler (Louise)
Mrs. Jerome Ohrbach [Mrs. Frederic Ingram] (Ingrid)
Mrs. Edwin W. Pauley (Bobbe)
Mrs. Gregor Piatigorsky (Jacqueline)
Mrs. Kenneth Pingree (Adrienne)
Miss Eleanor Pinkham
Mrs. Ernst H. Plesset (Polly)
Mrs. Gerald Evans Porter (Martha)
Mrs. Albert T. Quon
Mrs. Earl K. Russell (Maggie)
Mrs. George Vernon Russell (Mary)
Mrs. Charles I. Schneider (Barbara)
Mrs. Keesling Sesnon (Jaqueline)
Mrs. William T. Sesnon Jr. (Margaret)
Mrs. Evelyn Sharp
Mrs. Sidney Sheldon (Jorja)
Mrs. Sherman N. Shumway (Agnes)
Mrs. Forrest N. Shumway (Patsy)
Mrs. Elden Smith (Harriet)
Mrs. William French Smith (Jean)
Mrs. Kellogg Spear [Camilla Chandler Frost] (Mia)
Mrs. William E. Sprackling
Mrs. Robert Law Stafford
Mrs. Dennis C. Stanfill (Terry)
Mrs. Ray Stark (Fran)
Mrs. Jules Stein (Doris)
Mrs. Jane Lawler Stern
Mrs. Edward R. Valentine (Carol)

Mrs. Harry J. Volk (Marjorie)

Mrs. Richard R. Von Hagen (Lulu May)

Mrs. Glen E. Wallichs (Dorothy)

Mrs. Will Ward (Jane)

Mrs. John Wayne (Pilar)

Mrs. Harry H. Wetzel (Maggie)

Mrs. Warren B. Williamson (Alyce)

Mrs. Lorin H. Wilson (Annabelle)

Mrs. William Winans (Mignon)

Mrs. Roland Witte (Lee)

Mrs. Richard H. Wolford (Helen)

Mrs. William Wyler (Talli)

Mrs. Eugene L. Wyman (Rosalind)

Mrs. Charles E. Young (Sue)

Mrs. Edward K. Zuckerman (Posie)

Joined in 1970:

Mrs. Joseph D. Bain (Madeleine)

Mrs. Richard T. Barton (Patricia)

Mrs. Elmer Belt (Ruth)

Mrs. Morley Benjamin (Jan)

Mrs. Russell S. Bock (Suzanne)

Mrs. George Bortin (Virginia)

Mrs. Asa V. Call (Margaret)

Mrs. Edward C. Crossett (Elizabeth)

Mrs. Austin T. Cushman (Paula)

Mrs. Carl Deutsch (Roberta)

Mrs. Robert F. Erburu (Lois)

Mrs. Michael J. Fasman (Marjorie)

Mrs. Peter J. Fenchel (Donna)

Mrs. Ruth A. Finch

Mrs. Faye Goldstone

Mrs. Stewart S. Granger (Sue)

Mrs. Carl E. Hartnack (Roberta)

Mrs. Herbert S. Hazeltine Jr. (Frances)

Mrs. Harold M. Hecht (Betty)

Mrs. Edgar L. Janeway (Elizabeth)

Mrs. H. Bradley Jones [Mrs. Boyd T. Marshall] (Mary)

Mrs. Thorkild R. Knudsen (Valley)

Mrs. Frank G. Kranz (Eileen)

Mrs. J. Walter Lewy (Hazel)

Mrs. James B. Luckie (Dorothy)

Mrs. Vincent Lupo (Catherine)

Mrs. Ruth Koolish March

Miss Amanda May

Mrs. Maytor McKinley (Vari)

Mrs. Seely W. Mudd (Virginia)

Mrs. Gilbert C. Nee (Margaret)

Mrs. Robert D. Nelson (Georgia)

Mrs. Joseph R. Osherenko (Margo)

Mrs. Christopher G. Russell (Stella)

Mrs. Taft Schreiber (Rita)

Mrs. Daniel Schwartz (Natalie)

Mrs. Richard A. Stumm Jr. (Beatrice)

Mrs. Hayward Tamkin (Etta)

Mrs. Dorothy D. Trothcway

Mrs. Guy W. Wadsworth (Isabelle)

Mrs. George J. Wayne (Kyra)

Mrs. Francis M. Wheat (Nancy)

Mrs. Meredith Willson (Rosemary)

Joined in 1971:

Mrs. Carl G. Anderson (Lee)

Mrs. Shipley A. Bayless (Mary)

Mrs. Alphonzo Bell (Marian)

Mrs. Herman Blackman [Dr. Barbara Lockhart]

Mrs. Peter William Candy (Pauline)

Mrs. Aaron C. Clark (Laurel)

Mrs. William Lloyd Davis [Mrs. Terry Jastrow] (Anne Archer)

Mrs. Howard C. Deshong Jr. (Diane)

Mrs. Gloria Ellwood

Mrs. B.I. Forester [Mrs. Hal David] (Eunice)

Miss Gloria Gartz

Mrs. William Goetz (Edie)

Mrs. Stanley Goldblum (Marlene)

Mrs. Natalie Wood Gregson [Mrs. Robert Wagner]

Mrs. John Stevenson Griffith (Helene)

Mrs. David C. Grimes (Susan)

Mrs. Leo R. Grossman

Mrs. Argyle H. Gudie (Jane)

Mrs. Homer Hargrave

Mrs. Joseph W. Harper (Cecilia)

Mrs. Paul M. Hunter (Betty)

Mrs. James B. Isaacs (Marcia)

Mrs. Horace Kalik (Charlotte)

Mrs. Van Rensselaer Kelsey II (Nancy)

Mrs. Frank Kennedy (Rosalind)

Mrs. Alexander King

Mrs. Kent Landsberg (Carol)

Mrs. Jonathan Z. Larsen (Wendy)

Mrs. Jack I. Levin (Helen)

Mrs. Florence Mead MacKay

Mrs. Jerry Magnin (Erin)

Mrs. Thomas Aquinas Malatesta (Laurie)

Mrs. Thomas M. Malouf (Florence)

Mrs. Elise Mudd Marvin

Mrs. Walter Matthau (Carol)

Mrs. Neil S. McCarthy (Mary)

Mrs. Zubin Mehta (Nancy)

Mrs. Joseph D. Messler (Jane)

Mrs. William Miles [Ms. Tichi Wilkerson-Kassel]

Mrs. Lester Morrison (Rita)

Mrs. Henry T. Mudd (Ann)

Mrs. Robert F. Niven (Toni)

Mrs. John O'Melveny

Mrs. Armand Oppenheim (Gladys)

Mrs. Joan Palevsky

Mrs. Joseph H. Pollock (Helene)

Mrs. Alexander Saunderson (Louise)

Mrs. Arthur Schmutz (Betty)

Mrs. Sanford B. Schulhofer (Erna)

Mrs. Paul Selwyn (Joan)

Mrs. William N. Shattuck (Catherine)

Mrs. Norton Simon (Jennifer Jones)

Mrs. Charles P. Skouras Jr. (Diane)

Mrs. Chadwick F. Smith (Corinna)

Mrs. Nina B. Spencer

Mrs. Arthur Spitzer (Janice)

Miss Jill St. John

Mrs. Milton R. Stark (Judith)

Mrs. Vance L. Stickell (Betty Lee)

Mrs. Robert Paul Strub (Betty)

Mrs. Barry Taper (Barbro)

Mrs. Waller Taylor II (Jane)

Mrs. Judith S. Thomas

Miss Marlo Thomas

Mrs. John Truyens (Lilly)

Mrs. Thomas Wachtell (Esther)

Joined in 1972:

Mrs. Berle H. Adams (Lucile)

Mrs. William A. Baxter (Elizabeth)

Mrs. Welton Becket (Faye Kastner)

Mrs. Phil Berg (Leila)

Mrs. Harold D. Berkowitz (Beverly)

Mrs. Tom Berwald (Jean)

Mrs. George E. Brandow (Anita)

Mrs. C. Allan Braun (Marge)

Mrs. Elinor Mayer Bryden

Mrs. Joanne Carson

Mrs. Alfred P. Chamie (Betty)

Mrs. Pierre Claeyssens (Ailene)

Mrs. Loraine Miller Collins

Mrs. Richard Delauer (Ann)

Ms. Angie Dickinson

Mrs. Louise O. Dougherty

Mrs. Jack Drown (Helene)

Mrs. Charles G. Emery (Blanche)

Mrs. Isadore Familian (Shirley)

Mrs. Frank Feder (Joan)

Mrs. John W. Findlater (Helen)

Mrs. Montgomery R. Fisher (Joanne)

Mrs. Albert B. Glickman (Judith)

Mrs. Bonnie Grant

Mrs. Francis D. Griffin (Irene Dunne)

Mrs. Prentis Cobb Hale (Denise)

Mrs. Philip M. Hawley (Mary)

Mrs. Herbert Hezlep III (Elizabeth)

Mrs. James C. Hoover

Mrs. Aubrey H. Ison (Elizabeth)

Mrs. George Daniel Jagels Sr. (Margaret)

Mrs. Emmett Henry Jones

Mrs. William B. Keast (Harriet)

Mrs. Maureen A. Kindel

Mrs. Arnold S. Kirkeby (Carlotta)

Mrs. Kenneth Leventhal (Elaine Otter)

Mrs. Alan W. Livingston (Nancy Olson)

Mrs. Frederick P. Lyte (Marjorie)

Miss Alysia May

Anita Keiler May

Mrs. Glen McDaniel (Marilyn)

Mrs. Alathena Miller

Mrs. Virginia S. Milner

Sandra Moss

Mrs. Edmund R. Neil (Jessie)

Mrs. John R. F. Penido (Joyce)

Mrs. Robert E. Petersen (Margie)

Mrs. Morton Phillips (Abigail Van Buren)

Mrs. Robert W. Rand (Helen)

Mrs. John D. Roberts (Dian)

Mrs. Sanford B Schulhofer (Erna)

Mrs. Richard E. Sherwood (Dee)

Mrs. Frank Sinatra (Barbara)

Mrs. Henry E. Singleton (Caroline)

Mrs. Marvin Smalley (Sondra)

Mrs. Benjamin B. Smith (Dorothy)

Mrs. Thomas G. Somermeier Jr. (Lisa)

Miss Nancy J. Stolkin [Mrs. Thomas R. Vreeland Jr.]

Mrs. Walter V. Storm (Lisa)

Mrs. Leonard H. Straus (Dorothy)

Evelyn Stuart

Mrs. Donn B. Tatum (Vernette)

Miss Daphne Triphon

Mrs. Holmes Tuttle (Virginia)

Mrs. Eric B. Ward (Ann)

Mrs. Ray A. Watt (Nadine)

Mrs. Del E. Webb (Toni)

Mrs. Herbert Ziegler

Joined in 1973:

Mrs. Richard L. Anawalt (Patricia)

Mrs. Merle H. Banta (June)

Mrs. David Begelman (Annabelle)

Mrs. Thornton F. Bradshaw (Pat)

Mrs. William W. Buckwalter (Eleanor)

Mrs. Richard W. Call (Nancy)

Mrs. Coolidge Carter (Mary)

Mrs. James F. Chambers Jr.

Mrs. Louise Danelian

Mrs. Gordon Davidson (Judi)

Mrs. Glenn O. Dayton Jr. (Betty)

Mrs. Hyman Engelberg (Miriam)

Mrs. George N. Epstein (Lulu)

Mrs. Webb A. Everett (Marjorie)

Mrs. John Factor (Rella)

Mrs. Patrick J. Frawley Jr. (Gerry)

Mrs. Julian Ganz Jr. (Jo Ann)

Mrs. Leonard Goldberg (Wendy)

Mrs. Bram Goldsmith (Elaine)

Mrs. Arthur N. Greenberg (Audrey)

Mrs. Stephen Hinchliffe Jr. (Ann)

Mrs. Herbert L. Hutner (Juli)

Ms. Beverly D. Jefferies

Mrs. Harold Keith (Diane)

Mrs. Patricia Ketchum

Mrs. Frank E. Kilroe (Martha)

Mrs. James L. Knight (Barbara)

Mrs. Roslyn Kramer

Mrs. Henry L. Lee Jr.

Mrs. James F. Lesage (Ruth)

Mrs. Sidney Lushing (Lillian)

Mrs. Joseph Marx (Suzanne)

Mrs. Doris Mendenhall

Mrs. Howard C. Metzler (Ruth)

Mrs. Walter M. Mirisch (Pat)

Mrs. William H. Oldknow II (Dina)

Mrs. Alan J. Pakula (Hannah)

Mrs. George Ponty (Margaret)

Mrs. Anselmo L. Pozzo (Verle)

Mrs. David Raphel (Dina)

Mrs. Franklin Schaffner (Jean)

Mrs. G.T. Scharffenberger (Marion)

Mrs. Franklin H. Simmons (Rary)

Mrs. Robert Snyder (Judy)

Mrs. Aaron Spelling (Candy)

Mrs. Irving Stone (Jean)

Mrs. Elbridge Hadley Stuart Jr. (Marion)

Mrs. Dorothy A. Sweeney

Mrs. Robert H. Volk (Barbara)

Mrs. John Carl Warnecke (Grace Carl)

Mrs. William A. Wilson (Betty)

Madame King-Yan Wu (Sylvia)

Joined in 1974:

Mrs. Harry Bardt (Marguerite)

Mrs. Walter F. Beran (Speedy)

Mrs. Sidney F. Brody (Frances Lasker)

Mrs. John J. Burke (Nancy)

Mrs. William Chaikin (Anita)

Mrs. Clifford B. Cherry (Evelyn)

Mrs. Sherrill C. Corwin (Dorothy)

Mrs. Lester Deutsch (Betty Underwood)

Mrs. Charles E. Ducommun (Shirley)

Mrs. Ralph L. Edwards (Barbara)

Mrs. Samuel Firks [Mrs. Richard Brawerman] (Geri)

Mrs. Ruth Mahler Freshman

Mrs. John Charles Hazzard (Brena)

Mrs. James R. Hutter (Elizabeth)

Mrs. Russell E. Jordan (Hetty Joy)

Mrs. Edward Lasker (Cynthia)

Mrs. Edward Meltzer (Frieda)

Mrs. Barney R. Morris (Estelle)

Mrs. Roy E. Naftzger Jr. (Pauline)

Mrs. Cosimo Occhipinti (Dena)

Mrs. David Rose (Betty)

Mrs. Sydney Sher (Sylvia)

Mrs. Howard G. Smits (Gwen)

Mrs. Robert M. Sutton (Barbara)

Mrs. Elton F. Tomlinson (Dagmar)

Mrs. Murray Ward (Virginia)

Mrs. Gene M. Washburn

Mrs. Alva H. Wilson (Eleanor)

Miss Margery Wilson

Joined in 1975:

Mrs. Robert H. Adams Jr. (Elizabeth)

Mrs. John E. Anderson (Marion)

Mrs. Charles S. Arledge (Barbara)

Mrs. Virginia Babbitt

Mrs. Ross Barrett (Sherry)

Mrs. Robert D. Burch (Joann)

Mrs. Ralph Vincent Byrne (Patricia Duque)

Ms. Elizabeth Hofert Dailey

Mrs. Donald J. Davenport (Patricia)

Mrs. Carter De Haven (Bobby)

Mrs. Bosko De Jorjevic (Elizabeth Keck)

Mrs. William Henry Doheny (Onnalee)

Mrs. Mel Dorfman (Amelia)

Mrs. Paul A. Erskine (Georgianna)

Mrs. Louis Factor

Mrs. McIntyre Faries (Geraldyne)

Mrs. Charles W. Gates II (Elizabeth)

Ms. Roberta Haft

Mrs. Ernest W. Hahn (Jean)

Mrs. Fred J. Hayman (Gale)

Mrs. Doris Fields Heller

Mrs. Wayne M. Hoffman (Laura)

Mrs. James Russell Inman (Patricia Ann Barham)

Mrs. George H. Irvin (Rita)

Ms. Jacqueline Jardine

Mrs. Donald G. Kahn (Margery Jane)

Mrs. Barry Kaye (Carole)

Mrs. Richard H. Kealnge (Betty)

Mrs. James H. Kindel Jr. (Lupe)

Mrs. Hein I. Koolsbergen (Wendy)

Mrs. Andre Kostelanetz (Georgie)

Mrs. Albert D. Lasker (Mary)

Mrs. Marion Laurie

Mrs. Henri Lazarof (Janice Taper)

Mrs. Odell S. McConnell

Mrs. Ronald W. Miller (Diane Disney)

Mrs. C. Edward Miller (Nelda)

Mrs. Michael Minson (Launa)

Mrs. Everts Walker Moulton (Mary)

Mrs. Robert Muir (Georgette)

"Blue Ribbon is a prime example of how exposure, knowledge, and passion can inform and inspire people to think big."

–Michael Ritchie, Artistic Director, Center Theatre Group

Joined in 1980:

Mrs. Jackie Applebaum
Mrs. Sheldon I. Ausman (Sandy)
Mrs. Samuel Ayres III (Norma)
Mrs. Philip Barry (Patricia)
Mrs. V. Shannon Clyne (Pam)
Mrs. Charles E. Cord Jr. (Nancy)
Mrs. Jamie Del Amo (Jane)
Mrs. Mike Douglas (Genevieve)
Miss Diane Ruth Downey
Mrs. Serene L. Felt
Mrs. J. De Witt Fox (Evelyn)
Mrs. William Fremont (Eva)
Mrs. Maurice Hall (Adrienne)
Mrs. Charlton Heston (Lydia)
Mrs. Robert R. Hollman (Deloris)
Mrs. Frank L. Johnson (Frances)
Mrs. Francis X. Kane (Barbara)
Mrs. David Knight (Linda)
Mrs. Robert H. Lentz (Gloria)
Mrs. Kenneth F. Morgan (Betty)
Mrs. Peter O'Malley (Annette)
Mrs. Stephen R. Onderdonk (Kay)
Mrs. John L. Poole (Ms. Dorrie Braun)
Mrs. Allen E. Puckett (Marilyn)
Peggy Schaefer
Mrs. Franklin Simon (Sylvia)
Mrs. Joseph H. Stein Jr. (Joyce)
Mrs. Peter V. Ueberroth (Virginia)
Dr. Jane Woolley

Joined in 1981:

Mrs. John B. Allen (Carol)
Mrs. Roy A. Anderson (Betty)
Mrs. Ted L. Bartscherer (Betsy)
Mrs. Thomas L. Beckmen (Judy)
Mrs. Donald Sheridan Brady (Mary)
Mrs. Thomas J. Brant Jr. (Louise)
Mrs. Otis Chandler (Bettina)
Mrs. Frederick Clarey (Joanne)
Mrs. Joseph Connolly (Cindy)
Mrs. John C. Cushman (Ginny)
Mrs. Michael David (Angie)
Mrs. Irwin Deutch (Lynne)
Mrs. Gerald Dunitz (Maxine)
Mrs. David Foster (Jackie)
Mrs. Dominic Frontiere (Georgia)
Mrs. Jerry Godell (Gloria)
Mrs. Fred Hameetman (Joyce)
Mrs. John Harrigan (Barbara)
Mrs. Harold A. Held (Louise)
Mrs. Brent F. Howell (Elizabeth)
Mrs. Eli S. Jacobs (Joyce)
Mrs. Thomas F. Jones (Louise)
Alice Cantor
Mrs. William F. Kieschnick (Keith)
Mrs. John F. King (Pamela)
Mrs. George Konheim (Eve)
Mrs. Maury S. Leonard (Betty)
Mrs. Bruce L. Ludwig (Carolyn)
Mrs. Martin Manulis (Katherine)
Mrs. W.M. Marcussen (Barbara)
Mrs. Anthony A. Mastor (Sophie)
Ms. Asa Maynor
Mrs. William A. Mingst (Tally)
Mrs. George E. Mueller (Darla)
Mrs. R. Michael Murphy (Kathryn)
Mrs. James Neville (Jonnie)

Mrs. Herman Platt (Marjorie)
Mrs. Elisabeth N. Pollon
Ms. Paige Rense
Mrs. Arthur Rosenbloom (Nancy)
Mrs. Milton A. Rudin (Mary Carol)
Mrs. Lalo Schifrin (Donna)
Mrs. Charles Schneider (Dori)
Mrs. Vincent E. Scully (Sandra)
Mrs. Arnold Seidel (Joan)
Mrs. Gunjit S. Sikand (Margarete)
Mrs. Donald Simon (Judy)
Mrs. Joseph Sinay (Ruth)
Mrs. Kyhl S. Smeby (Mary)
Mrs. Norman F. Sprague III (Marianne)
Mrs. Russell Stromberg (Claudia)
Mrs. Bernard Tabakin (Mary)
Mrs. Michael L. Tenzer (Jacqueline)
Mrs. Walter D. Williams (Joan)
Mrs. Harold M. Williams (Nancy)
Mrs. Henry F. Winkler (Stacey)
Mrs. Charles B. Witt Jr. (Colette)
Mrs. Ruth E. Yablans
Mrs. Richard D. Zanuck (Lili)

Joined in 1982:

Mrs. Roy H. Aaron (Teri)
Mrs. Robert Anderson (Diane)
Mrs. Joseph E. Baird (Anne Marie)
Mrs. Joanne Baizer
Sharon Swanton Black
Mrs. Irwin Buchalter (Ethel)
Miss Carol Burnett
Mrs. Waldo Burnside (Jean)
Mrs. Laurie O'Connell Champion
Mrs. Timothy A. Childs (Terri)
Miss Anne Lloyd Crotty
Mrs. Marvin Davis (Barbara)
Mrs. Kirk Arnot Day (Elizabeth Sprague)
Mrs. Michael D. Eisner (Jane)
Mrs. Gary J. Freedman (Nancy)
Judge Carol Boas Goodson
Mrs. Marvin Goodson (Mae)
Mrs. Samuel M. Grossman (Peggy)
Mrs. Alexander Haagen III (Betty)
Mrs. Charles McKey Hart (Alice)
Mrs. Reginald Howard (Lois)
Mrs. Thomas J. Hutchison Jr. (Carolyn)
Susan H. Jeffries
Mrs. Joseph J. Keon Jr. (Sally)
Mrs. Daniel A. Kirsch (Shelby)
Mrs. Ignacio E. Lozano Jr. (Marta)
Mrs. James M. Luckman (Alison)
Mrs. Garry Marshall (Barbara)
Mrs. Fred W. O'Green (Mildred)
Mrs. Lawler Reeves (Eleanor)
Mrs. Daniel H. Ridder (Frani)
Ms. Elberta Ellis Riley
Mrs. Herbert Y. Rosenblum (Joyce)
Mrs. Albert S. Ruddy (Wanda)
Mrs. Francis E. Schlueter (Estelle)
Mrs. E.L. Shannon Jr. (Ruth)
Dr. Roseann Slotkin
Ms. Lisa Specht
Mrs. Jerry Weintraub (Jane)

Joined in 1983:

Mrs. Robert Abell (Constance)
Ms. Tamara Asseyev
Mrs. Irving Axelrad (Ethel)
Linda H. Peck Babbitt
Mrs. John B. Clayburgh (Ruth)
Mrs. Robert Colman (Celeste Yarnall)
Mrs. Joseph H. Coulombe (Alice)
Mrs. Earle E. Crandall (Arlette)
Mrs. Veronica Pastel Egelston
Mrs. Robert A. Heebner (Jacqueline)
Mrs. Desmond J. Hinds Jr. (Nancy)
Mrs. Glen A. Holden (Gloria)
Mrs. Robert G. Hunt (Sally)
Mrs. James H. Jacobson (Rudi)
Mrs. Thomas Kardashian (Joan)
Mrs. Judith Karns
Mrs. Louis L. Kelton (Elsa)
Mrs. Lester B. Korn (Carolbeth)
Mrs. Richard B. Lippin (Ronnie)
Mrs. Robert F. Maguire III (Susie)
Mrs. Harry Maron (Bert)
Mrs. Bruce A. Meyer (Raylene)
Mrs. Paul A. Mitchell (Ingrid)
Mrs. Sidney R. Petersen (Nancy)
Mrs. George A. Roberts (Jeanne)
Mrs. Kenny Rogers (Marianne)
Mrs. Rockwell Schnabel (Marna)
Mrs. John W. Shumway (Susan)
Mrs. Robert Stack (Rosemarie)
Mrs. R. Paul Toeppen (Dorothy)
Mrs. Donald Tronstein (Arletta)

Joined in 1984:

Mrs. Gordon M. Anderson (Liz)
Mrs. Henry Berger (Jayne)
Mrs. Andrew Blackmore (Ruth)
Mrs. Eli Broad (Edye)
Mrs. B. Gerald Cantor (Iris)
Mrs. Samuel Colt (Eleanore Phillips)
Mrs. Margaret A. Coryell
Mrs. Nicola S. Dantine (Niki)
Mrs. Jerome Fein (Joy)
Ms. Barbara Foley
Mrs. Happy I. Franklin (Frances)
Mrs. Russell Goldsmith (Karen Mack)
Mrs. Michael Gould (Karen)
Mrs. Melvin Guthman (Laura)
Mrs. J. Michael Hennigan (Phyllis)
Mrs. Orion L. Hoch (Nan)
Ms. Judith K Hofer
Mrs. Elliott S. Horwitch (Adrienne)
Mrs. John F. Hotchkis (Joan)
Mrs. Irving J. Karp (Ruth)
Mrs. Peter Keller (Margaret)
Mrs. Jennings Lang (Monica)
Mrs. Thomas E. Larkin Jr. (Margaret)
Mrs. David C. Martin (Mary)
Mrs. Charles D. Miller (Carolyn)
Mrs. Robert Glenn Morris (Linda Kay)
Mrs. Leon Morton (Diane)
Mrs. Anne Marie Moses
Mrs. Bob Ray Offenhauser (Kathy)
Mrs. Gerald Oppenheimer (Virginia)
Mrs. Ellis Ring (Frances)
Mrs. Albert Sacks (Claire)
Mrs. Leonard Shapiro (Annette)
Mrs. Ronald B. Smith (Carol)

Mrs. Laurence G. Sterling (Terry)
Mrs. Steven Chapman Thomas (Judith)
Barbara Hale Thornhill
Mrs. Alexander Varga (Olive)
Mrs. Howard E. Varner (Mary)
Mrs. Nancy Weakley
Mrs. Marlin F. Wilson (Alice)

Joined in 1985:

Mrs. Richard F. Alden (Marjorie)
Mrs. Rudy Dean Belton (Kathryn Klinger)
Mrs. Mark Buchman (Angela)
Mrs. Eugene J. Burton (Betye)
Mrs. Arnold Cohen (Carol)
Mrs. Louis C. Cohen (Joan)
Mrs. Gary Collins (Mary Ann Mobley)
Mrs. William Conti (Shelby)
Mrs. William Lloyd Davis (Teran)
Mrs. Dennis Eisenberg (Jayne)
Mrs. Henry K. Elder III [Mrs. Stan Chambers] (Virginia)
Mrs. Burton N. Forester (Nanette)
Mrs. Maynard Franklin (Charlotte)
Mrs. James M. Galbraith (Peggy)
Mrs. Stephen Gans (Elizabeth)
Mrs. Bernard R. Garrett (Carolyn)
Mrs. Bernard Gelson (Ann)
Mrs. Doreen Glick
Mrs. Henry Gluck (Arline)
Mrs. Mark S. Greenfield (Susan)
Mrs. Robert Lee Humphreys (Marie)
Mrs. Lawrence F. Irwin (Sachi)
Mrs. Franklin R. Johnson (Anne)
Mrs. Paul R. Kanin (Sally)
Ms. Patricia Jean Kennedy
Mrs. Robert Kirkpatrick (Nadine)
Mrs. Gilman Kraft (Ruth)
Mrs. Louis L'Amour (Kathy)
Ms. Lilly Lee
Mrs. Howard Lipstone (Jane)
Mrs. Ruben F. Mettler (Donna)
Mrs. Paul A. Miller (Marjory)
Mrs. Richard F. Miller (Suzanne)
Mrs. James P. Miscoll (Inge)
Mrs. Howard B. Morrow (Joyce)
Mrs. Peter W. Mullin (Pam)
Mrs. Norman S. Namerow (Barbara)
Mrs. Ted Orden (Hedy)
Mrs. Russell B. Pace Jr. (Margaret)
Ms. Diane Perkins (Papo)
Mrs. Kristoffer Popovich (Jane)
Mrs. Allen Questrom (Kelli)
Mrs. Bruce M. Ramer (Ann)
Mrs. Lupe J. Rodriguez (Lucia)
Mrs. Harvey Rosen (Donna)
Mrs. David P. Ruderman (Judy)
Mrs. William Schulte (Marilyn)
Mrs. Sanford Sigoloff (Betty)
Mrs. Dimitri Skouras (Patti)
Mrs. Peter Bercut Smith (Becky)
Mrs. Michael Srednick (Lee)
Mrs. Peter Strauss (Susan)
Mrs. Burt Sugarman [Mrs. Jamal Ali-Ahmad] (Kathryn Davis)
Mrs. Robert Sully (Jeanne)
Mrs. Charles B. Thornton Jr. [Mrs. Michael W. Harahan] (Nancy)
Mrs. Louis Warschaw (Carmen)

Mrs. Walter Weisman (Sheila)
Mrs. Ben Winters (Elaine)

Joined in 1986:

Mrs. Martin Albert (Ann)
Dr. E. Jane Arnault [Dr. E. Jane Arnault-Factor]
Mrs. Stanley Black (Joyce)
Mrs. John R. Bradley (Eileen)
Mrs. Anthony Brent (Tisha)
Mrs. Rhonda Fleming Mann Carlson
Mrs. Edward M. Carson (Nadine)
Ms. Jacqueline Cotsen [Ms. Jacqueline Brandwynne]
Mrs. Diane Forester
Mrs. Charles S. Franklin (Susan)
Mrs. Stanley M. Freeman (Annetta)
Mrs. Emese Tardy-Green
Mrs. Warner Heineman (Anne)
Mrs. Warner W. Henry (Carol)
Mrs. David F. Kamin (Donna)
Mrs. Morton Kay (Beverly)
Mrs. Stuart M. Ketchum (Carrie)
Mrs. Raymond Kurtzman (Lynette)
Mrs. Dorothy D. La Due
Mrs. J. Terence Lanni (Debbie)
Mrs. Robert S. Marx (Gilda)
Mrs. Maurice Meyers (Kathy)
Mrs. Vincente Minnelli (Lee)
Mrs. Katherine Keck Moses
Mrs. Frederick M. Nicholas (Joan)
Mrs. Beatrix Padway
Mrs. James Porter (Faith)
Mrs. Robert Recht (Susan)
Mrs. Carl M. Rheuban (Debby)
Mrs. Thomas E. Riach (Joan)
Mrs. Eugene Robbins (Mitzi)
Mrs. Charlotte Rosenberg
Mrs. Brad Rosenberg (Tanya)
Ms. Adelyne N. Ross
Mrs. Joseph A. Saunders (Lorraine)
Mrs. Clifford E. Schiffer (Kelly)
Mrs. Bruce Sherr (Margaret)
Mrs. William E.B. Siart (Noelle)
Mrs. Robert H. Smith (Loretta)
Mrs. John D. Stolkin (Kathy)
Mrs. Bill Todman Jr. (Karen)
Mrs. Stanford Weiss (Marcia)
Mrs. Jack Douglas Whitehead (Helen)
Mrs. Milton Widelitz (Misty)
Mrs. Abram Charles Zukor (Dayle)

Joined in 1987:

Mrs. Paul Alter (Shirley)
Mrs. Thomas G. Armstrong (Martha)
Mrs. Peter K. Barker (Robin)
Mrs. Lodwrick M. Cook (Carole)
Mrs. Royce Diener (Jennifer)
Mrs. A. Redmond Doms Jr. (Mary)
Mrs. Charles F. Elkins (Eva)
Mrs. Norman Feintech (Evelyn)
Mrs. Howard S. Freedland (Kathy)
Mrs. Ernest A. Goldenfeld (Marion)
Mrs. Verna Harrah
Mrs. Sue Kaplan
Mrs. Sandra Krause (Sandy)
Mrs. Douglas Mancino (Carol)
Mrs. Beth Pressman

Mrs. Harry Roman (Ruth)
Mrs. Dickinson Crosby Ross (Gabriele)
Mrs. Richard A. Schulman (Marcia)
Mrs. David Wilstein (Susan)
Mrs. Martin J. Wolff (Donna)
Mrs. Richard Ziman (Lynn)

Joined in 1988:

Mrs. Harold E. Applebaum (Betsy)
Mrs. John Charles Bedrosian (Judy)
Mrs. Robert McKim Bell (Lisa)
Ms. Kay Brown
Mrs. George A. Brumder (Marilyn)
Mrs. Gregory R. Brundage [Mrs. Hardy Thomas] (Mary Beth)
Mrs. Ian Campbell (Nancy)
Mrs. William Clossey (Margaret)
Mrs. Roderick C. Devin (Pat)
Mrs. Richard K. Eamer (Eileen)
Mrs. James D. Farley (Mary Kay)
Mrs. O.L. Frost Jr. (Nell)
Ms. Betty Goodwin
Mrs. Homer M. Harvey (Gloria)
Ruth L. Harvey
Mrs. Byron Hayes Jr. (Deanne)
Mrs. Boyd Hight (Mary Kay)
Elizabeth Levitt Hirsch
Mrs. Irving Kellogg (Evelyn)
Mrs. Ronald H. Malin (Roni)
Ms. Kathleen Marshall
Mrs. John Martens (Bridget)
Mrs. Sherman Mazur (Michelle)
Mrs. David McIntyre (Norma)
Mrs. Robert L. Mettler (Susan)
Mrs. Reese Milner II (Mary)
Mrs. Jack Mishkin (Nancy)
Mrs. Victor Moss (Nancy)
Mrs. Gerald L. Parsky (Robin)
Mrs. Arthur F. Pizzinat (Julie)
Mrs. Rosalind Pritikin
Mrs. Ken Rickel (Nancy)
Mrs. Harold Roach (Betty)
Mrs. Carl W. Robertson (Sue)
Mrs. Pam Rubin
Mrs. David N. Schultz (Dona Haynes)
Mrs. Richard A. Shortz (Jan)
Mrs. Bartine A. Stoner (Madeleine)
Mrs. Donald M. Tallarico (Judy)
Mrs. Thomas R. Tellefsen (Debbie)
Mrs. Michael E. Tennenbaum (Suzanne)
Mary Harms Weir
Mrs. Joseph Wolf (Marilyn)
Ms. Maureen A. Wright

Joined in 1989:

Mrs. Joseph V. Bentley (Barbara)
Mrs. David Bianchi (Cherry)
Mrs. William J. Bird (Toni)
Mrs. Leonard Bovee (Iris)
Mrs. Robert L. Burkett (Sally)
Mrs. Henry Burroughs (Jennifer)
Ms. Marcia Caden
Mrs. A.J. Carothers (Carol)
Mrs. Alan Casden (Nancy)
Mrs. Henry Chesler (Eunice)
Mrs. James A. Collins (Carol)
Mrs. Michael J. Connell
Mrs. Kenneth R. Corday (Sherry)

Mrs. Robert A. Daly [Nancy Daly Riordan]
Mrs. Maurice J. DeWald (Carolyn)
Mrs. Daniel L. Dworsky (Sylvia)
Mrs. Edward C. Ellis (Clarice)
Mrs. Jerrold Felsenthal (Judy)
Ms. Maria P. Ferrer
Mrs. Gordon Freshman (Timi)
Mrs. Charles W. Fries (Ava)
Ms. Carol Sapin Gold
Mrs. Craig L. Gosden (Jane)
Mrs. Milton Gottlieb (Brindell Roberts)
Mrs. Virginia Heinz
Mrs. Donald A. Hicks (Mary Lou)
Ms. Rosanna Hill
Mrs. Arthur Houston Jr. (Thelma)
Helene Berk Irvin
Mrs. Richard Kayne (Suzanne)
Mrs. Michael Kazanjian (Virginia)
Mrs. Russell D. Keely (Carlotta)
Mrs. Gerald W. Labiner (Suzanne)
Mrs. Vasilios Lambros (Helen)
Ms. Jeanne K. Lawrence
Mrs. Alan D. Levy (Abby Jane)
Mrs. Randall Lewis (Janell)
Ms. Genevieve McSweeney
Mrs. Marc Nathanson (Jane)
Mrs. Michael Niven (Susan)
Mrs. James O'Hern (Nina)
Mrs. Michael Ovitz (Judy)
Mrs. Roberta Pawlak
Mrs. Matthew Rapf (Carol)
Mrs. Ronald Reagan (Nancy)
Mrs. Edward S. Renwick (Gloria)
Mrs. Thomas Revy (Nancy)
Mrs. Eugene S. Rosenfeld (Maxine)
Mrs. Norman C. Ross (Gloria)
Ms. Astrid H. Rottman
Mrs. Patricia Rucker [Mrs. John F. Nickoll]
Mrs. Irwin Russell (Suzanne)
Mrs. Larry Sade (Joan)
Mrs. Peter Schweitzer (Winne)
Mrs. Robert E. Shor (Sukey)
Mrs. Burt Sugarman (Mary Hart)
Mrs. Linda May Suzar
Susan Knobel Talesnick
Mrs. Frank B. Thompson (Joan)
Mrs. Robert H. Tourtelot (Susan)
Mrs. Howard L. Tullis (Ruth)
Ms. Jessica Vitti
Mrs. Robert Wagner (Carolyn)
Ms. Elka Weiner
Mrs. Charles Wick (Mary Jane)
Mrs. Norman B. Williamson (Cici)

Joined in 1990:

Mrs. Bettina Bancroft
Mrs. George N. Boone (MaryLou)
Norma L. Clark
Mrs. Robert D. de Palma (Maryann)
Mrs. Leonard Fischer (Shirley Levine)
Mrs. Andrew Galef (Bronya)
Constance Towers Gavin
Mrs. Herbert Glaser (Sharon)
Mrs. Bert W. Greynald (Corina)
Janet C. Jones
Mrs. Marvin Jubas (Fern)
Mrs. Bruce E. Karatz [Janet Dreisen Rappaport]

Mrs. Susan Levich
Mrs. John M. Liebes (Gail)
Mrs. Bruce P. McNall (Jane)
Mrs. Allen E. Paulson (Madeleine)
Mrs. Jerry Perenchio (Margaret)
Mrs. Davis Pillsbury (Patricia)
Mrs. Charles Reilly (Barbara)
Mrs. Lois Rosen
Gaile Gray Ryan
Mrs. Philip S. Salet (Willie)
Mrs. Marvin J. Shapiro (Sophie)
Mrs. Robert Shrum (Marylouise Oates)
Mrs. Robert Silverstein (Anita)
Mrs. Milan D. Smith [Mrs. Arnold C. Kirkeby] (Maidee)
Ms. Susan Knobel Talesnick
Mrs. Yukiyasu Togo (Misako)
Mrs. Kenneth Tokita (Sandy)
Ms. Hope Warschaw
Mrs. Stephen F. Weiner (Claire)
Mrs. Lewis R. Weintraub (Roberta)
Mrs. Richard A. Wilson (Patty)
Cynthia Sikes Yorkin
Mrs. Henry A. Yost (Cindi)

Joined in 1991:

Mrs. Kiyohiko Arafune (Asako)
Maralee Beck
Mrs. Allan Burns (Joan)
Mrs. Robert Dickerman (Madeline)
Mrs. Herbert D. Eagle (Babe)
Mrs. Hugh Hinton Evans Jr. (Lynn)
Beverly Firestein
Pilar Munoz de Garrigues
Mrs. Leonard A. Goldman (MeraLee)
Mrs. Sheldon M. Gordon (Christy)
Ms. Amy Grauman (Danziger)
Mrs. Anthony P. Hatch (Lenore)
Bailey R. Kanin
Mrs. John B. Kilroy Sr. (Chantal)
Mrs. Howard Ladd (Lara)
Dr. Marguerite Marsh
Mrs. William G. McGagh (Sarah)
Ms. Sylvia J. Newman
Mrs. Lawrence Powell (Joyce)
Mrs. Tracy Price (Ellen)
Mrs. Fredric N. Richman (Arleen)
Deborah F. Rutter
Mrs. Clive M. Segil (Larraine)
Roberta Silbert
Victoria Mann Simms
Mrs. Jerry Snyder (Joan Parker)
Mrs. Richard A. Stone (Lona)
Mrs. Stuart Taylor (Gladys)
Mrs. Daniel M. Tellep (Patricia)
Mrs. Ira Yellin (Adele)

Joined in 1992:

Mrs. Stephen Ackerman (Jane Vollstedt)
Mrs. Mario Antonini (Marisa)
Mrs. Ronald Aubert (Bobbe)
Mrs. Ralph E. Bailey (Harriet)
Mrs. Robert C. Baker (Cheryl Ferraro)
Mrs. Peter Baldwin (Terry)
Mrs. Ira Cohen (Patricia Meder)
Mrs. Paul J. Conn (Sally)

Cynthia Coulter (Mrs. James J. Bardwil)
Mrs. Joan Fitzgerald DuBois
Mrs. Mark J. Epstein (Louise)
Mrs. Larry Flax (Joan)
Mrs. Mark Foster (Claudia)
Mrs. Robert B. Garber (Marilyn)
Mrs. Mohammad A. Gharavi (Jennifer)
Mrs. Sylvan Goldinger (Cathy)
Joanne D. Hale
Mrs. Jack H. Halgren (Jane)
Mrs. Mary Hayley
Mrs. Harlan Herzberg (Barbara)
Mrs. Bruce Hochman (Harriet)
Ms. Maria Hummer [Maria Hummer Tuttle]
Mrs. William Keck II (Susan)
Mrs. Kent Kresa (Joyce Anne)
Mrs. Arthur Levine (Lauren Leichtman)
Dr. Elizabeth J. Lu
Mrs. James A. Middleton (Victoria)
Mrs. Rupert Murdoch (Anna)
Melody Y. Nishida
Mrs. John A. Osterkamp (Terre)
Vicky L. Patton
Ms. Barbara Platt
Mrs. Frank E. Raab (Sally)
Mrs. Charles R. Redmond (Bette)
Mrs. Frederic Rheinstein (Suzanne)
Mrs. Nelson C. Rising (Sharon)
Mrs. Dale Rosenbloom (Kathleen)
Mrs. Richard Rosenfield (Esther)
Mrs. Arthur H. Shapiro (Bernice)
Gloria Sherwood
Evelyn Carol Spound
Regina G. Steiner
Mrs. Richard Swarz (Sandy)
Donna Frame Tuttle (Donna F. Tuttle Elmore)
Mary Beth Van Dine
Mrs. Richard E. Waldron (Patricia)
Mrs. Richard Weintraub (Liane Manshel)
Mrs. Bruce G. Willison (Gretchen)
Mrs. Joe Winter (Alison)
Diane Wittenberg

Joined in 1993:

Mrs. James R. Andrews (Gail)
Paulette Blumenthal
Mrs. Mike Bowlin (Martha Ann)
Lucia Hidalgo Brady
Mrs. Douglas A. Brengel (Lynn)
Linda Traub Brittan
Helene Briskin Brown
Mrs. Martin Cooper (Shelley Kirkwood)
Mrs. Derek Dawson (Sheila)
Mrs. Paul S. Ebensteiner (June)
Maggie Coleman Edwards
Mrs. Julian Elliott (Carolyn)
Mrs. Ronald M. Florance (Elaine)
Ingrid E. Hanzer
Mrs. Christopher B. Hemmeter Sr. (Patricia)
Mrs. Donald Hirsch (Darrelle)
Ms. Marcia Wilson Hobbs
Mrs. Alan Joelson (Yasmina)
Mrs. Russell L. Johnson (Mary)

Pamela Anne Karner
Mrs. Cleon Knapp (Betsy Wood)
Mrs. Stephen Krantz (Judith)
Barbara T. Lindemann
Mrs. David C. Lizarraga (Pricilla)
Mrs. J. Thomas McCarthy [Mrs. Franklyn Kostlan] (Kathleen)
Mrs. James W. McCord (Jann)
Mrs. David D. Miller (Denyse)
Mrs. John J. Morrissey III (Wendy Stark)
Mrs. James L. Perzik (Judi)
Ms. Nancy Revy
Mrs. Edwin Lee Rodgers (Gayle)
Mrs. Richard K. Roeder (Fritzy)
Mrs. Arna Saphier
Mrs. Michael W. Sheller (Geannie Holden)
Mrs. James A. Shuemaker (Heather)
Mrs. S. Donald Sims (Gail)
Mrs. Roger M. Sullivan (Jayne)
Mrs. David Sydorick (Ginny)
Mrs. Michael Viner (Deborah Raffin)
Mrs. Thomas W. Wathen (Janna)

Joined in 1994:

Mrs. Richard D. Aldrich (Joan)
Mrs. Connie Austin
Mrs. Steven Bernfeld (Susan McLane)
Mrs. Ann Berns
Mrs. Harold Borden (Ruth)
Mrs. Donald R. Boulanger (Jasmina)
Mrs. William R. Burkitt (Paulette)
Sandra McNutt-Comrie
Mrs. Michael Dart (Nettie)
Mrs. Stuart Davis (Mary)
Mrs. Nancy Neal Davis
Mrs. Leslie Dornfeld (Grazia)
Jean C. Fair
Mrs. Peter B. Fodor (Barbara)
Mrs. Michael J. Fourticq (Janet)
Mrs. Jerald Friedman (Judi)
Miss Patricia Fry
Mrs. Graeme A. Gilfillan (Elizabeth)
Mrs. Edgar F. Gross (Marcy)
Mrs. Fred Hayman (Betty Endo)
Carol Jaffe
Mrs. Felix Juda (Helen)
Shelley Z. Kadison
Mrs. Gerald L. Katellsaperste
Mrs. Robert Kramer Jr. (Rosemary)
Mrs. Thomas F. Kranz (Travis)
Mrs. Leo Krashen (Julia)
Mrs. Zev L. Lapin (Susan)
Ms. Shari Leinwand
Mrs. John Light (Sharon)
Elizabeth H. Lowe
Mrs. Elliott Maltzman (Rusty)
Mrs. Kenneth Mariash (Donna)
Mrs. Anthony P. Mazzarella (Susan)
Ms. Janet McCloud
Mrs. John E. McGovern (Elizabeth)
Mrs. John P. McNicholas (Diana)
Patricia McQueeney
Dr. Vicki Mercer
Mrs. Thomas Midgley IV (Sandy)
Mrs. Richard Milholland (Bonnie)
Mrs. Stephen D. Miller (Jeanne)
Mrs. Mace Neufeld (Helen)

Christine H. Newman
Mrs. Arnold Palmer (Patsy Juda)
Mrs. A. Barry Patmore (Carole)
Linda Ann Halverson Pennell
Karen Kay Platt
Mrs. Arnold Porath (Anne Hyde)
Mrs. Stewart A. Resnick (Lynda)
Mrs. Robert Rifkind (Stephanie Barron)
Susan Rothenberg
Mrs. Daniel P. Ryan (Pat)
Tawny Lee Sanders
Mrs. Martin Schechter (Barbara)
Mrs. William E.B. Siart (Laura)
Arline Susswein
I.H. Sutnick
Mrs. Terry Turkat (Roberta)
Elinor Turner

Mrs. Kenneth Russak (Grace)
Mrs. Shinji Sakai (Ryuko)
Mrs. Irving Singer (Ruth)
Mrs. David T. Smith (Norma)
Mrs. Joachim Splichal (Christine)
Mrs. Morton Steinberg (Bobbye)
Ms. Louise Taper
Marilyn Trattner
Betsy Roberts Ulf
Nancy A. Ziehl

Joined in 1996:

Margie Miller Baum
Mrs. Albert Broccoli (Dana)
Mrs. Ronald Brown (Linda)
Mrs. Alan Casden (Susan)
Nadine Chaves

Amanda Stonnington
Suzanne Tito
Leslie F. Vermut
Anna Marie Warren
Mrs. Howard Zelikow (Marcie)

Joined in 1997:

Mrs. Donald Alschuler (Lynne)
Margaret Sheehy Collins
Margit Sperling Cotsen
Karen Bedrosian Coyne
Kathryne Dahlman
Diane Jeanne Dykema
Marcia Harrow
Mary Ann E. Hunt-Jacobsen
Mrs. Ronald Karsin (Lynne)
Mrs. Kenneth Lopaty (Barbara)

Zee Marzec
Mrs. John R. Miller (Juli)
Synne Hansen Miller
Mrs. Patricia Paley Neu
Mrs. Howard R. Panosian (Vera)
Mrs. Richard C. Schnell (Annette)
Grazyna Simon
Mrs. M. Melvin Sirota (Bette)
Ms. Babette Sobel
Ms. Cathleen M. Tyner
Mrs. Ernest Wilson (Inez)

Joined in 1999:

Dr. Phyllis Abrams
Lois Driggs Aldrin
Elizabeth N.Q. An
Mrs. Thomas Barrat (Sherry)

Joined in 2000:

Jackie Banchik
Mrs. Donald E. Benson
Dr. Toni Bernay-Porrath
Mrs. Shane Broumand (Judy)
Mrs. Anthony F. Daly Jr. (Carla)
Ms. Gabrielle Davis
Mrs. Anthony Canzoneri (Cindy)
Mrs. Daniel Feldman (Diane)
Mrs. Lawrence N. Field (Eris)
Ms. Darlene Fogel
Donna Garber
Mrs. Sol Gindoff (Lydia)
Marion Goldenfeld
Julie Goldsmith
Mrs. Samuel H. Halle II (Courtney)
Mrs. Ghada Irani

"The sight of thousands of kids singing and dancing on the Music Center Plaza is unforgettable; you can imagine the joy they feel!"
–Grant Gershon, Music Director, Los Angeles Master Chorale

Ellen Lee Goldsmith (Goldsmith-Vein)
Angelle Grace Wacker
Hon. Kim McLane Wardlaw
Mrs. Roscoe C. Webb Jr. (Lydia)
Barbara J. Wilkinson
Mrs. Robert Wiviott (Sharon)
Mrs. James Young (Brooke)

Joined in 1995:

Mrs. Louis Adler (Sharon)
Mrs. George T. Aratani (Sakaye)
Mrs. Philip L. Ball (Terry)
Sandra Bosley
Mrs. Alton J. Brann (Anna)
Mrs. Mark Taylor Burger (Susan Garton)
Mrs. Edward E. Clark (Alicia)
Mrs. Richard H. Diehl
Mrs. Irwin S. Field (Helgard)
Mrs. Charles Forbes Jr. (Margie)
Roya Megnot Geiderman
Lisa D. Hansen
Mrs. John Indrieri (Jo Ann)
Ms. Sandra Kimberling
Mrs. Jay Livingston (Shirley)
Mrs. Mario Mory (Phyllis)
Mrs. Philip M. Neal (Meredith MacRae)
Barbara J. Parsky
Mrs. Guy Perry [Mrs. Burton Monsach] [Linda Glass]
Mrs. Peter Petrafeso (Debbie)
Sandra Post
Dallas Price-Van Breda
Mrs. Larry Rabineau (Harriet)
Joyce Rey
Hon. Vicki Reynolds

Mrs. Larry Cohen (Paulette)
Mrs. Jan Turner Colburn
Ms. Kimberly Corman
Ms. Kathleen D. Crane
Mrs. James Cross (Sue)
Mrs. Larry J. Dagley (Norma)
Mrs. R. Thomas Decker (Denise)
Mrs. James Econn (Christine)
Mrs. Stanley N. Goff (Elaine)
Mrs. Don Granger (Lisa)
Mrs. Rockell N. Hankin (Lisa)
Laurie Hartigan
Mrs. Angelika Hederer
Mrs. Akio Hirato (Terry)
Mrs. Sydney M. Irmas (Audrey)
Mrs. Guy Juillard (Joelle)
Mrs. Douglas Kahn (Margaret Carter)
Mrs. Ronald A. Katz (Madelyn)
Mrs. David Kelton (Lenny)
Lauren King
Rini Kraus
Mrs. Mark Liberman (Karen)
Mrs. Anthony Mansour (Amanda)
Mrs. Phillip Matthews (Lois)
Mrs. Clifford A. Miller (Judith)
Mrs. Herman C. Millman (June)
Therese P. Mothorohood
Mrs. Ronald Nelson (Joyce)
Mrs. Samuel Oschin (Lynda)
Mrs. Robert D. Paulson (Robin)
Annette Pearson
Ms. Penelope C. Roeder
Julia N. Sanchez
Mrs. David Saperstein (Suzanne)
Mrs. Piero Selvaggio (Stacy)
Ms. Marjorie Skouras
Eva Suzanne Stern

Helen R. Mars
Mrs. Michael R. McCormick (Christine)
Mrs. Todd M. Morgan (Cheri)
Mrs. Peter W. Mullin (Merle)
Mrs. Murray Ozer (Beverly)
Mrs. Francis R. Palmer III (Robyn)
Mrs. M. William Perel (Rochelle)
Kathleen Scheinfeld
Mrs. Joel Simon (Nancy)
Mrs. Albert Snider (Joan)
Mrs. Valerie Sobel
Kimila W. Ulrich
Mrs. Aimee A. Walker (Rick)
Dr. Melinda Fassett Welles
Mrs. Derk Zimmerman (Susan)

Joined in 1998:

Mrs. Lawrence S. Ades (Annette)
Kathryn A. Ballsun
Marjorie Binder Beradino
Mrs. Robert F. Berger (Janet)
Ms. Adele Binder
Mrs. Robert C. Bogert (Trudy)
Mrs. Stephen Bollenbach (Barbara)
Mrs. John T. Cardie (Phyllis)
Mrs. Richard D. Colburn (Lisa)
Ames Crawford Cushing
Ms. Lynn M. De Groot
Mrs. William K. Doyle (Cheryl)
Mrs. Michael R. Forman (Patricia)
Aliza Karney Guren
Mrs. Steven H. Hammer (Martha)
Mrs. Gail Hankin
Joyce Eisenberg Keefer
Pearle Rae Levey

Mrs. Les Biller (Sheri)
Mary Jane Boggs Barger
Phyllis F. Easton
Margaret D. Eberhardt
Mrs. Sidney R. Eshleman (Kristen)
Mrs. Arnold Gale (Stephanie)
Ms. Lisa Hagen
Ms. Pamela J. Hoefflin
Dr. Alice S. Huang
Jane Hulick
Linda Janger
Mrs. Donald M. Koll (Kathleen)
Mrs. Daniel Lautman (Jo-Ann)
Mrs. David Licht (Diane)
Mona Tromble Mapel
Mrs. Owen Miller (Janice)
Mrs. Lawrence P. Murphy (Paula)
Marti Oppenheimer
Mary Pattiz
Cheryl Petersen
Mrs. Barry Pressman (Sandra)
Mrs. Nathan Prusan (Lilian)
Mrs. Herbert Rappaport (Evy)
Mrs. Charles Read (Eileen)
Mrs. Arthur L. Rosenbaum (Sandra)
Mrs. Stan Rothbart (Miriam)
Marcella Ruble
Ms. Audre Slater
Roslyn Holt Swartz
Mrs. Julian Weinstock (Lois)
Luanne C. Wells
Mrs. Richard Wolf (Nancy)
Mrs. Edwin G. Zalis (Rosalie)

Gina Knox
Constance York Lynch
Mrs. Paul MacCaskill (Laurie)
Mrs. Robert E. Meyer (Britt)
Gail Wiley Oppenheimer
Mrs. Herbert M. Poncher (Sheila)
Mrs. David Richardson II (Carol)
Mrs. Wayne H. Smith (Barbara)
Mrs. Andrew M. J. Steinhubl (Marie)
Dr. Patricia Trenton
Nancy Van Tuyle
Mrs. Lee H. Wagman (Barbara)

Joined in 2001:

Mrs. Robert M.L. Baker Jr. (Bonnie)
Mrs. Javier Baz (Colleen)
Pamela Beck
Mrs. Eric Binder (Shannan)
Mrs. Alexander Cappello (Linda)
Mrs. Christophe Choo (Gabrielle)
Mrs. Edmond R. Davis (Ruby)
Ms. Jane Dorian
Mrs. Jules Fogel (Jacqueline)
Diane Glazer
Ilene C. Gold
Patricia Dunn Grey
Ms. Carolyn Hotchkis
Mrs. Richard M. Kagan (Julie)
Donanne Kasikci
Charlotte Lane
Mrs. Steven Maslauski (Laurie)
Kacey Doheny McCoy
Mrs. Douglas H. McKellar Jr. (Dana)
Mrs. Michael Miller (Hayley)
Mrs. John Moller (Elizabeth)
Ms. Dawn Moore

Carole Curb Nemoy
Mrs. Edmund Olivier de Vezin (Ellen)
Mrs. John Puerner (Elizabeth)
Ms. Jacalyn Ross
Mrs. Pete Rugolo (Edye)
Mrs. Fred Sands (Carla)
Mrs. Charles J. Schatz (Bambi)
Linda Schlesinger
Mrs. Manfred Simchowitz (Jennifer)
Mrs. Ronald P. Spogli (Georgia)
Mrs. Charles Stephens (Amy)
Mrs. Robert G. van Schoonenberg
   (Sandra)
Mrs. Mert Wallen (Inger Osteraa)
Mrs. Stuart Weiser (Anna)
Mrs. Ian White-Thompson (Barbara)
Ms. Kathleen M. Wiltsey

Joined in 2002:

Beatrice Bennett
Mrs. David G. Booth (Suzanne)
Linda J. Bowling
Robin Rosenzweig Broidy
Mrs. Marvin M. Chalek (Susan)
Ms. Diane Conn
Mrs. Carolyn H. Denham
Mrs. Ralph Ehrenpreis (Jennifer)
Mrs. Andrew K. Forthmann Jr. (Lori)
Ms. Kara Fox
Kari Fraser
Ann Marshall Holder
Mrs. Louis Kwong (Angelina)
Sherry Lansing
Mrs. Stephen Liu (Machi)
Victoria L. McCluggage
Mrs. Willem Mesdag (Lisa)
Mrs. James Oates (Debra)
Mrs. Geoff Palmer (Anne)
Cathryn Palmieri
Jill M. Reilly
Mrs. Richard Rogers (Elizabeth)
Mrs. George Rosenthal (Karen)
Mrs. Alan I. Rothenberg (Georgina)
Mrs. Ronald D. Sugar (Valerie)
Mrs. W. Clarke Swanson Jr.
Stephanie Spencer Tellefsen

Joined in 2003:

Rachel Ault
Avery B. Barth
Mrs. Ze'ev Drori (Carolynne)
Kimberly Marteau Emerson
Colleen Evans
Mrs. Blaine P. Fetter (Linda)
Gerri Lee Frye
Mrs. Pierre Josefsohn (Marguerite)
Mrs. Martin Katz (Kelly)
Lindsey C. Kozberg
Mrs. Harold Lancer (Dani)
Mrs. Gene C. McCaffery
Mrs. Ed McMahon (Pam)
Sandra M. Milstein
Ms. Katherine O'Malley
Ricki Ring
Mrs. Jeffrey Rosenthal (Gayle)
Sandra Rudnick
Mrs. Chuck Russell (Patti)
Mrs. James N. Shelton II (Sarah)
Mrs. Michael Spitzer (Rosalind)

Mrs. Mike Stoller (Corky)
Lynda Lamberti Stubblefield
Mrs. Thomas Walper (Maritia)

Joined in 2004:

Mrs. Philip Alford (Elizabeth)
Mrs. Michael D. Barker (Janice)
Maria Bell
Leah S. Bergman
Mrs. James F. Brennan (Barbara)
Mrs. Anthony H. Browne (Gay)
Alison Bryan Crowell
Kathleen Erickson
Mrs. Stan Freberg (Hunter)
Lisa D. Janian
Mrs. J.B. Ladd (Doris)
Mrs. Ned R. Nelsen (Janice)
Carolyn Powers
Mrs. Barry Smooke (Julie)
Marilyn Stein
Cathy Stone
Elizabeth Pavlova Tito
Mrs. Joseph M. Weller (Carol)
Andrea Greene Willard

Joined in 2005:

Margot Armbruster
Jill C. Baldauf
Mrs. Howard Baldwin (Karen)
Tracey Boldemann-Tatkin
Lynn A. Booth
Jacqueline Burdorf
Dr. Anita Artstein-Dunsay
Alexandra Dwek
Marcia Ehrlich
Quinn Ezralow
Linda Freund
Gia Luisa Honnen-Weisdorn Esq.
Mrs. J.D. Hornberger (Nancy)
Ellen Lee
Mrs. Marty Pasetta (Elise)
Mrs. Edward Pellegrini (Stephanie)
Terri Smooke
Gloria Strasburger
Mrs. John A. Sussman (Donna)
Heidi G. Widelitz
Mrs. Jonathan Williamson (Shannon)

Joined in 2006:

Mrs. William T. Baumann (Katherine)
Ms. Janice E. Bini
Ms. Christina Dickson
NancyJane Goldston
Ms. Janis B. Hague
Terri Kohl
Mrs. Donald A. Kurz (Hope)
Sara Kutler
Bernadette Leiweke
Claudia Lin Margolis
Mrs. Theodora Rifkin
Mrs. Mark Siegel (Christina)

Joined in 2007:

Kevin Cartwright
Ms. Jeanne S. Friedman
Susan Gersh
Linda Joyce Hodge

Mrs. Marv Hoffman (Marni)
Kathleen Holthouse
Tania Norris
Mrs. Leslie A. Pam (Ann)
Mrs. Bennett C. Pozil (Marni)
Mrs. Paul Rubenstein (Suzanne)
Elizabeth Segerstrom
Mrs. Gerock Swanson (Frances)

Joined in 2008:

Susan Christie
Mrs. Nancy Garen
Ms. Marasuba T. Granderson
Susan L. Harris
Lisa Hubbard
Mrs. Stuart Korshak (Louise)
Mallory Lewis
Sonia Randazzo
Mrs. Dayna Shulman
Rosa Kendall Sinnott
Lynelle Wagner

Joined in 2009:

Lucinda L. Alden
Nancy de Brier
Elizabeth A. Doran
Ms. Susanne Meline Francis
Mrs. William Hammerstein (Marcy)
Sally Kiernan
Mrs. George D. Kirkland (Frances)
Mrs. Alejandro Ortiz (Rachel)
Diane B. Paul
Ms. Renwy Graves Pittman
Mrs. Helen M. Posthuma
Mrs. Kenneth G. Riley (Erika)
Kimberly L. Shah
Carol Smith
Ms. Victoria Ann Sofro
Chantal Mastey Stern
Ms. Gretchen Garrett Valentine
Ms. Lucy Wolff

Joined in 2010:

Kathrine Forest Baxter
Mrs. Arthur Cook (Nevada)
Ms. Maryann Gold
Carol Goldsmith
Mrs. Valerie Foster Hoffman
Mrs. Jack Kavanaugh (Leslie)
Mrs. Monica Kirchner
Mrs. Peter D. Mallory (Susan)
Kay Klein Pick
Carol Swanson Price
Wendy Knudsen Pylko
Susana Mercedes Scroggins
Mrs. Jonathan Veitch (Sarah)
Stephanie Germain Vinokour

Joined in 2011:

Christine M. Adams
Dr. Geraldine Alden
Victoria Briggs Bagdasarian
Ms. Suzonne Bass
Mrs. James Birdwell (Nancy)
Ms. Judy Chang
Mrs. Joyce Chernick
Mary Lallande

Barbara Marcus
Ms. Jolie T. Nelson
Ms. Ariela Shani
Annabelle Weston Shulman
Ms. Sue Tsao

Joined in 2012:

Holly A. Baril
Suzanne Bonafede
Ms. Susan Brauneiss
Ms. Ellen Calcaterra
Christine Alexandra Chiu
Brenda Chandler Cooke
Kimberly Ann Evans
Mrs. Cynthia Fields (Cindy)
Susan Finkelman
Kathryn M. Johnson
Dr. Susan Kendall-Bell
Dr. Anu Leemann
Francine Light
Jody Fink Lippman
Christine Lowe
Barbara Mack
Marie Elena Maclennan
Kim Merritt
Mary Helen Michel
Mrs. Pamela Mohn
Lea Porter
Lillian Postaer
Ms. Desiree Badr Samuels
Stephanie Vahn
Mrs. S. Vickar (Simone)
Carol Ann Warren

Joined in 2013:

Laurel Beebe Barrack
Mary Blodgett
Lisa Clark
Laurie Cohen
Donna Econn
Mrs. William Fain (Jennifer)
Ms. Debra Fine
Kiki Ramos Gindler
Karen L. Heilman
Nancy Elkins Hinds
Cindy Leuty Jones
Jacqueline McNally Kruse
Ellen Lipson
Jennifer Bellah Maguire
Celeste Pinto McLain
Michele McMullin
Cynthia S. Monaco
Lisa Neipris
Mrs. Thomas Rauth (Pat)
Ms. Sharon Shelton
Tracy B. Smith
Julie Spira
Mrs. Joseph A. Sposato (Suzanne)
Gillian Wagner
Marilyn Ziering

"The arts have always—and will always—
play a critical role in society
and childhood education."

–Esa-Pekka Salonen, Music Director Laureate, Los Angeles Philharmonic Orchestra

Acknowledgments

I knew from the instant I met with three savvy and strong women—Carla Sands, Betty Leonard, and Donna Wolff—to discuss the project they envisioned, that I wanted to be part of it. *Blue Ribbon: Amazing Women, Powerful Giving* is more than a history of a philanthropic group that has held sway over the Los Angeles cultural scene for nearly fifty years—it is a social history of the city.

The book allowed me to reconnect with many of the dynamic Blue Ribbon members who had made a huge impression on me when I was a *Los Angeles Times* social reporter during the 1980s and early '90s—especially Joanne Kozberg who enlisted me to write the first official account of the group for its twentieth anniversary. Interviews I conducted then with the group's founders and early presidents provided lifelines for me as an author in 2013.

I also happily reunited with my Stanford classmates Harry and Denise Hardrè Chandler, who were the very first people I called on when I set to work. To me, Harry and his brother Norman were California royalty in college—tall, blond, handsome, and their father Otis published the newspaper that landed on my parents' driveway every morning. Never in a million years could I have foreseen writing about their formidable grandmother, Dorothy Buffum Chandler. The book could not exist without Harry's trove of knowledge and family photographs, both of which he freely shared.

All of the Blue Ribbon past presidents I interviewed were extraordinarily gracious, as were Andrea Van de Kamp, Lenore and Bernie Greenberg, Judi and Gordon Davidson, Dona Kendall, Lois Erburu, Alyce Williamson, Wallis Annenberg, Helen Bing, Ginny Mancini, Walter Mirisch, Dody Waugh, Annette O'Malley, Alice Avery, Marcia Hobbs, Peggy Grauman, Harlyne Norris, Edythe Broad, Judy Beckman, Carol Henry, Maxine Dunitz, Eunice David, Julie Goldsmith, Lucy Wolff, Lynelle Wagner, Joan Boyett, Suzy Boyett, Suzanne Marx, Laurie Salvatori Champion, Katie Wetzel Murphy, Cindy Dowell, Ruth Jones, who passed away shortly after we spoke; and Diane Disney Miller, who talked about her own Blue Ribbon memories and shared wonderful recollections of her mother, Lillian.

I can't praise book-project co-chairs Donna Wolff and Betty Leonard enough. They steered this ship from start to finish. It's one thing to imagine a book and quite another to make it a reality—none of us had any idea how challenging this would be. We all talked and emailed daily and around the clock (weekends and holidays included!) to get the job done. They saw their primary responsibility as making sure that Blue Ribbon was properly portrayed, and they tirelessly weighed every word and scrutinized every picture to see that happen.

Blue Ribbon is fortunate to have a president like Carla Sands. Throughout, she was

Betty Leonard, left, and Donna Wolff co-chaired this book project.

steadfast in her support, delegated decisions when appropriate, offered astute critiques when asked, and always, always was encouraging.

I simply could not have functioned without Associate Director Erin Haley in The Blue Ribbon Office, (who, on top of everything, organized the historic roster, a massive task) and archivist Michael Mocciaro; they both not only filled in dozens and dozens of blanks, but always did so immediately and with a smile. Director Erin Cockrill also kindly sought out answers to my many questions, no matter how complex, whenever necessary. Music Center archivist Julio Gonzalez and Major Gifts Officer Cheryl Brown were of invaluable assistance.

As for the beautiful book in hand, credit goes to photo researcher Eric Lynxwiler, a sleuth in every sense who has an innate gift of choosing images with a sense of history, drama, and vitality; and to Art Director Hilary Lentini—who is elegant and forward-thinking at the same time—of the Los Angeles firm, Lentini Design and her graphic designers Leanna Hanson and Tory Black. But all of our work would have been completely useless were it not for the wise and steady leadership—and seamless editing talent—of Publishers Paddy Calistro and Scott McAuley of Santa Monica's Angel City Press. The bright commentary of Assistant Editor Niree Perian provided perspective for us all.

Everyone involved is especially indebted to Frank Gehry who opened up his heart and put pen to paper to create the original cover art work.

The Dorothy Chandler Papers held by the UCLA Library Special Collections at the University of California, Los Angeles were indispensable to me. Not to be forgotten are the books which informed me,

including *The Music Center Story: A Decade of Achievement 1964-1974*, edited by James W. Toland; *Music Center of Los Angeles County: Celebrating Twenty-Five Years 1964-1989,* by Mark Swed; *The Powers That Be,* by David Halberstam; *Inventing L.A.: The Chandlers and Their Times* by Bill Boyarsky; *Dreamers in Dream City*, by Harry Chandler; *Privileged Son: Otis Chandler and the Rise and Fall of the L.A. Times Dynasty*, by Dennis McDougal; and *Ronnie and Nancy: Their Path to the White House, 1911-1980*, by Bob Colacello. Lastly, society pages in the *Los Angeles Times* provided a cherished record of Blue Ribbon high points through the years.

Betty Goodwin, 2013

Photography and Image Credits

Author Betty Goodwin, photography researcher Eric Lynxwiler, and the Blue Ribbon wish to thank everyone who has contributed art to this book. Except as noted below, all images and ephemera are from the collection of the Blue Ribbon. Every attempt has been made to credit photographers for their work; any oversights are unintentional and will be corrected in future editions. We are extremely grateful to the following artists and sources:

Frank Gehry: cover, from the drawing for *A Rose for Lilly* fountain at Walt Disney Concert Hall; 140, drawing for Walt Disney Concert Hall. **Gary Leonard:** 121. **Harry Chandler Collection:** 11, 20 top and bottom; 21, 22 upper right; 24, 27, 28, 30, 37. **Los Angeles Philharmonic Archive:** 76, 99 bottom. *Los Angeles Times* **Photographic Archive, Department of Special Collections, Charles E. Young Research Library, UCLA:** 25 and 46 upper left (Mary Frampton); 53 and 54 (Harry Chase); 61 (Bill Varie), 68 and 72 top and bottom (Tony Barnard); 73 and 75 bottom left (Mary Frampton); 77 and 83 left (Harry Chase); 83 upper and lower right; 84 (Joe Kennedy); 85 and 86 top (Larry Bessel); 86 bottom (Kathleen Ballard); 87 top (Larry Bessel), 108 (Tony Barnard). **Los Angeles Public Library Photo Collection:** 17 (Herald-Examiner Collection); 59 (Security Pacific National Bank Collection). **Mancini Family:** 145 right. **MPTV Images:** 13 (©1978 Wallace eawell/mptvimages.com). **Music Center Archives:** 2 (Tim Street Porter); 8 (Henry Salazar); 14-15 (Otto Rothschild); 22 upper left; 22 bottom; 23, 33, 57, 124 upper left, 131, 138, 140 (Tim Street-Porter), 143 upper right (Christodoulou); 143 second from lower right; 143 bottom right; 144, 153.

Blue Ribbon: Amazing Women, Powerful Giving
By Betty Goodwin | Design by Lentini Design

Copyright © 2013 The Blue Ribbon | ISBN-13 978-1-62640-011-5

Library of Congress Cataloging-in-Publication Data is available

Published by The Blue Ribbon | A custom publication of Angel City Press, Santa Monica
Printed in Korea